Three to Win

JAMES E. ADAMS

Gospel Publishing House/Springfield, Mo. 65802

02-0906

© Copyright 1977 by the Gospel Publishing House,
Springfield, Missouri 65802. Adapted from *Soul Winning* by
Robert L. Brandt, ©1964 by the Gospel Publishing House.
All Rights reserved. Library of Congress Catalog Card
Number 77-072255. ISBN 0-88243-906-5. Printed in the
United States of America.

A teacher's guide for group study with this book is available
from the Gospel Publishing House (32-0176). ISBN 0-88243-176-5

Contents

Contents

1

Rewards in Doing

Freely Giving

Bone-tired members of the Sierra Madre Search and Rescue Team rolled into town with the dawn. It had been a successful mission—scrambling across crumbling granite cliffs in the inky night, seeking a lost hiker. One rescuer fielded the question: "You do this for free? Why?"

"I'm offering what I know to help people out," he replied. "A person can't go through life without donating something."

Donate. I like that. Freely give.

God freely gave His Son. Christ came to seek and to save the lost; to give His life to rescue them. But after His resurrection He met the 11-man search-and-rescue team He had trained, now occupied with the mundane pursuits of life—fishing.

"Lovest thou me more than these?" He asked Peter.

Usually we focus on Peter squirming under the thrice-repeated question. But Peter searched the face of the Son of God. He saw love and compassion for him and for all mankind. He never forgot. From that moment he was one with the Master. He spent his life seeking the lost; telling them about the great salvation Christ provided (Acts 4:12).

We cannot look into the eyes of Jesus. But His question remains. It insistently seeks an answer.

5

Do we really love Him? Do we love whom He loves? That's the crux. To love Him is to serve Him. To serve Him is to continue His search for the lost. To tell them, as Peter did, that there is salvation in none other than Jesus Christ. To say: "The gift of God is eternal life through Jesus Christ our Lord" (Romans 6:23).

The Wonder of Salvation

Everybody ought to know who Jesus is. Sinful men should learn that His great salvation is a wonderful, transforming experience—supernatural—a miracle of divine grace.

A missionary to the Meo people of Indochina had been using their word *pang*, meaning "to save." But he just wasn't satisfied. *Pang* was a fairly common word that somehow failed to convey the deeper meaning of salvation.

Then one day a Meo woman fell into a rain-swollen stream. The missionary jumped in and pulled her out.

"Ah," said an onlooker, "you *tse* her."

"You mean I 'pang' her, don't you?" the man of God asked quickly.

"Oh, no," said the Meo. "You *tse* her. That means you saved her by putting yourself in the same danger."

That one word made a great difference in the attitude of the Meo people to Christianity. The God of the Christians came to "tse" them. He really loved and cared for them!

No man can be saved unless he begins to see the wonder of divine love and grace. The eternal Son of God put himself in man's place; suffering to save him and give him eternal life.

Christ himself could not get His disciples to comprehend His earthly mission. Only Mary of Bethany grasped and believed the Lord's announcements of His coming death and resurrection.

Love and wonder filled Mary's heart. She broke the alabaster box of ointment and anointed her Lord. She testified to endless ages that Jesus is the Lamb of God who takes away the sin of the world. Man criticized her, but Jesus said: "She hath done what she could: she is come aforehand to anoint my body to the burying" (Mark 14:8).

Not everyone gives testimony to his faith. Some criticize those who do. But every Christian has the responsibility to do what he can to witness to the wonder of redeeming love and grace.

Nice People Are Lost

No man can be saved unless he knows he's lost.

Joe operates a lathe in Shop 4. What a guy! He sparks the company softball team with hits in the clutches and with chatter. But with all his talk, he never mentions God or anything spiritual.

Sue runs a sewing machine in the dress factory. A truly delightful girl! Time studies and the pressures for production can't keep her from breaking the routine with a smile and a cheerful word. But she never speaks about church.

You missed the bus. Spike picked you up and delivered you to your work site and absolutely refused remuneration. Wish he could find something good to say about acquaintances though.

What do Joe, Sue, and Spike have in common? They are kind and helpful. They also belong to earth's largest company. They have not accepted salvation through Jesus Christ. They're lost. We know it. Do they? Has anyone told them "all have sinned; all fall short of God's glorious ideal" (Romans 3:23, *The Living Bible*)?

Few people are "rotten to the core." There's something commendable about practically everyone you know. But kindness and commendable traits are no sure indications that an individual loves Jesus Christ.

On the other hand, close association with anyone undoubtedly reveals some rough spots. Personality flaws or failure to mention God in conversation do not necessarily signify that a person is bound for hell.

Christians make mistakes and repent. Believers are heaven-bound because they believe the gospel and have accepted Christ as their Saviour.

Nice people are lost because, for some reason or excuse, they have not repented of their sins. Fine friends and fellow employees need our testimonies.

Common Ground

"Whatever a person is like, I try to find common ground with him so that he will let me tell him about Christ and let Christ save him" (1 Corinthians 9:22, *The Living Bible*).

Christians find "common ground" on the job. They can if they keep a Bible handy. And use it.

Sam usually read his Bible during the lunch hour. One day a rough and witty fellow employee winked at others sitting around and dropped down beside him. "Whatcha reading, Sam?" he asked. "A love story?"

"Yeah. In a way." Sam turned a page or two and continued, "What do you make of this?"

Then he read the story of the Prodigal Son. Chances were, the witty fellow had never heard it. "Sounds like me," he admitted seriously. But then, flippantly—"It sure isn't like my old man!"

"But it is like God," Sam said quietly.

That stopped the witty one. Days passed, and he began to find occasion to stop at Sam's bench during the lunch hour. Soon, eating lunch together became a daily occurrence. Now his wit has been turned into a spiritual asset. He directs a boys' camp and serves as a Christian counselor.

These men were opposites and they still are. But both serve God and man because one sought and found common ground with the other.

If you or I had been in Sam's shoes, would the results have been the same? How do we react when a person tries to bait us before an audience? Are we slow to speak?

Sam played it cool. Unruffled. Turning the pages of his Bible unhurriedly gave him opportunity to whisper a prayer and to calm his spirit. Then the Holy Spirit prompted him to say the right words at the right moment. That's why Sam found common ground and a receptive hearer. That's why the hearer found Christ.

The Persuader Must First Be Persuaded

A Florida high school teacher was lecturing his students on the physiological effects of smoking cigarettes. Opening a fresh pack, he lit one to demonstrate the brown stain smoke would leave when blown through a handkerchief.

Suddenly it struck the science teacher. That smoke was staining the alveoli in *his* lungs. The nicotine was poisoning *his* delicate capillaries. Later he said: "While talking to my students, I convinced myself. I still had 19 cigarettes in the pack, but I quit smoking then and there."

The apostle Paul was convinced that a judgment day was coming for the lost. He also knew every believer must some day give account of himself at the judgment seat of Christ. Like the apostle Peter, he may well have thought: "If the righteous scarcely be saved, where shall the ungodly and the sinner appear" (1 Peter 4:18)? And he wrote: "We know what it means to fear the Lord, and so we try to persuade men" (2 Corinthians 5:11, TEV).

He convinced himself that it was his responsibility to persuade sinners to accept Christ.

Usually the most effective salesman is himself sold on his product. He is convinced he's doing others a favor by persuading them to buy it.

A recipient of manifold spiritual blessings, who but the Christian should be sold on what Christ offers? He offers salvation—without money and without price. What greater bargain can be offered? He offers His abiding presence and His Word to light the way. The balm of Gilead for physical well-being and the guidance and quickening of the Holy Spirit are the believer's. It's a natural! Every Christian can be a born (again) salesman; a persuader of men.

Persuaded, but Not Changed

Sometimes persuasion is not enough. A man convinces himself he needs a new automobile. He goes to the display room remembering the deal he got 2 years before. Somehow it hasn't registered that inflation has hit the auto industry as well as the supermarket. The deal turns him off. So, he decides to just get new tires and a tune-up. "After all, my car's still in good condition," he concludes.

Persuaded? Yes and no. He didn't change models.

Ninety-five percent of the people queried in a poll said they believed in God. But asked whether or not their religion in any way affected their politics or their business, 55 percent replied, "No." Only 25 percent admitted any connection between their religious beliefs and the conduct of their daily lives.

Most of those people were persuaded about the existence of God. (Devils are too—they tremble.) But that conviction made no change in the lives of the majority in the poll.

Every week in churches across the land pastors invite sinners to accept Christ. Convinced of their need, some raise their hands. But when the appeal is given to come to the altar, many remain in their seats. The cost is too great.

Persuaded? Up to a point. Sometimes persuasion does not move people to change their cars, their lives, or their destinies.

In witnessing to an individual, finding common ground is a good beginning. Spirit-led conversation that persuades him he needs Christ is commendable. But at that point the mission is half accomplished. God wants the discourse to culminate in repentance, prayer, and a change in heart and life—conversion.

As Little Children

A godly man testifies: "My son led the way."

For several years he attended an Assembly of God Sunday school. Conviction gripped his heart more and more. To escape it and the pricks of conscience, he began to leave his 7-year-old son in Sunday school, picking him up at the conclusion.

Finally, after Sunday school one day, the boy said: "Daddy, I got saved this morning. Did you?" It was the last straw. That night the family attended church. Father and mother gave their hearts to Christ and fully surrendered their lives to Him.

Jesus said: "Unless you repent (change, turn about) and become like little children [trusting, lowly, loving, forgiving] you can never enter the kingdom of heaven at all" (Matthew 18:3, *The Amplified Bible*).

Conversion is an about-face. "Old things are passed away; behold, all things are become new" (2 Corinthians 5:17). Conversion doesn't transport a person into his second childhood; rather, it delivers him from the old attributes of selfishness, skepticism, pride, and malice.

11

Recent educational research with small children suggests that by the age of 4, development of creative curiosity and the ability to deal with new concepts may be crucially influenced. And by the age of 5, our intellectual development is 50 to 75 percent complete.

Conversion, the new birth, is to become like little children. It helps a person to grasp new spiritual concepts, to grow in grace and in the knowledge of Christ, and to become wise as serpents and harmless as doves—or as little children.

The conversion of the lost is the goal of everyone who gives testimony to the saving grace of Jesus Christ.

By My Spirit, Saith the Lord

Eyes popped one Sunday morning as Red, the town tipsy, his wife, and little daughter entered the church. The pastor preached an inspired sermon. Some said the message brought the alcoholic to the altar. Others felt that God answered his wife's prayers. She thought little Jennifer's plea for daddy to take her to church had broken his heart. And only Red knew how disturbed he had been since the previous Friday. A fellow employee had said: "Red, may I ask you a question? You just quoted John 3:17 almost word for word. Since you know Christ came not to condemn you but to save you, how can you continue to reject Him?"

Red still reminds his fellow employee of his unanswerable question. But who can tell which human agent influenced him most?

The Holy Spirit brought it all to his remembrance that day, and Red was converted. From drunkard—to Sunday school teacher—and eventually, to church elder.

Jesus said that after His departure He would send His disciples another Comforter. He continued: "And when he [the Holy Spirit] is come, he will reprove [convict] the world of sin" (John 16:8).

12

Since the Day of Pentecost, dedicated saints have depended on the guidance and power of the Holy Spirit. Scripture passages have been brought to the remembrance of even unlearned and ignorant men in such logical, convincing ways that multitudes have been "pricked in their heart" (convicted of their sins). Excuses have vanished. They have cried, "What shall we do?" And the answer has come to all men everywhere, "Repent ye and be converted."

A witness without the Holy Spirit is but a voice crying in the night. The Holy Spirit has the invitation and the answer for sinners today. And He speaks through the lips of modern soul winners.

Togetherness

"All things are of God, who hath reconciled us to himself by Jesus Christ, and hath given to us the ministry of reconciliation" (2 Corinthians 5:18). Webster defines *reconcile* as: "To bring together; to unite; to restore to friendship." God counted reconciliation an accomplished fact with the death and resurrection of His beloved Son.

The need for reconciliation does not necessarily indicate that both parties are at odds with one another. A mother does not require persuasion to forgive a wayward son. When he wishes to be reconciled, it is his move. She welcomes him with open arms.

The Lord is not as some willful sinners have pictured Him: a vengeful God, waiting to vent His wrath upon His hapless creation at the least provocation. Instead, He stands with outstretched arms. He loves everybody. He is not willing that any should perish, but that all should come to repentance.

The ones who need to be reconciled are sinners. They are as sheep who have gone astray, following the path that seems right to them. And Christ, the Good Shepherd, still seeks the one lost sheep.

This is our message, for God has committed unto us the ministry of reconciliation. And it is good news to this generation standing in the shadow of Armageddon. The suicide rate among teenagers and young adults is truly alarming. Inflation, strikes, pollution, violence—where will it all end? People are deeply concerned. Men's hearts are failing them for fear.

To reconcile sinners to God; to pray together and see bitterness, tension, and worry yield to the peace of God which passeth understanding; and to fellowship with these newborn ones and help them grow in grace—this labor of love is its own reward in this life.

And for the life to come the Lord promises: ''They that be wise shall shine as the brightness of the firmament; and they that turn many to righteousness, as the stars for ever and ever'' (Daniel 12:3).

2

Reflecting Christ

Evangelist Billy Graham called it "one of the greatest sermons ever preached to me."

In Madras, India a Hindu student said, "I would become a Christian if I could see one."

Billy Graham further commented: "And when he said that, he was looking at me."

Most sinners do not put it so bluntly. Nevertheless, they expect Christians to manifest the attributes of Christ in their daily lives.

How would we feel if a similar remark were made to us? Would it put us on the defensive? It shouldn't. Would we fumble in our minds for a comment, an excuse, an answer? We shouldn't. We are only sinners saved by grace. And we need the grace of God every moment of every day. A reminder of our fallibility should simply increase our desire to become more Christlike and increase our determination to depend on Him.

In the small booklet "The Practice of the Presence of God" by Brother Lawrence, he wrote: "I know my weakness, which is so great that if He left me one moment to myself I should be the most wretched man alive. And yet I know not how He can leave me alone, because faith gives me as strong a conviction as sense can do that He never forsakes us until we have first forsaken Him."

15

Brother Lawrence believed and accepted Christ's promise: "I am the vine, ye are the branches. He that abideth in me, and I in him, the same bringeth forth much fruit; for without me ye can do nothing" (John 15:5). And that spells it out. Alone we will fail. In and with Christ all things are possible to him who believes. We can and should be Christlike.

Run the Race

The apostles were reminded of their weaknesses. On one occasion Paul found it necessary to withstand Peter "to the face, because he was to be blamed" for a division between Jews and Gentiles (Galatians 2:11).

Although Paul "stood up to" Peter, he did not think he "had it made." He admonished himself, the Ephesians, and us to put off the old man and to put on the new. He practiced self-control, bringing his body into subjection, lest after preaching to others he himself should be a castaway (1 Corinthians 9:27).

Paul further emphasized the need of self-control and cooperation with Christ in the Christian life by comparing it to a race.

Kipchoge Keino came from a farm village in Kenya, East Africa. A Christian runner, he trained for the 1968 Olympics to be held in Mexico City. Just a few days before his first Olympic race he was stricken with malaria.

Did Kip panic? Turning to his Bible he read: "Let us run with patience the race that is set before us" (Hebrews 12:1). And he said to his teammates, "I have no strength to run by myself. But God gives me quietness and confidence."

Then Kip lost the 10,000-meter race. But over a week later he had regained strength and was ready for the 1500-meter event.

16

In that race Kip ran against Jim Ryun, holder of the record for the distance. Kip passed him and won the race, setting a new Olympic record of 3:34.9. Attacked by malaria, he trusted Christ, kept his cool, and won the prize, the gold medal.

Paul endured his thorn in the flesh. He was attacked, beaten, and stoned. Yet he won great victories for Christ. Then he summed it up: "Not as though I . . . were already perfect: but I follow after, . . . I press toward the mark for the prize of the high calling of God in Christ Jesus" (Philippians 3:12, 14). He persisted in the race and won.

Grow in His Likeness

The winner in Christ—the soul winner—will experience health and sickness, victories and defeats, ups and downs. Every one of these, whether good or ill, should make him more like Christ. As Paul put it, we can "grow up into him in all things . . . unto a perfect man, unto the measure of the stature of the fullness of Christ" (Ephesians 4:15,13).

In David Wilkerson's book *Jesus Person Maturity Manual* (Glendale, CA: Gospel Light/Regal Publications, 1971), he tells about a converted acid freak who had returned to the old life. The youth said: "I was really zapped by the Spirit. I was really up on Christ. But it was a bummer. Nobody told me about temptations, about the devil trying to bring me down. Somebody wasn't honest with me."

Nobody told this young man that One greater than the world and Satan abode in his heart. He could abide in Christ by faith and could grow up into Him.

Jesus used the vine as an example for a reason. This Christian life of abiding and growing is like the life process in the vine. It doesn't struggle to produce fruit. It accepts the nutrients from the earth. With the buffeting of the wind it simply thrusts its roots wider and deeper.

To the one who is abiding and growing in Christ, the winds (temptations) beat upon the vine. But he is protected; hidden with Christ in God.

Paul wrote about growing unto a perfect man. The title of David Wilkerson's book mentions the same thing, maturity. Paul is not speaking of the ultimate perfection of the Christian when he enters heaven. For he admitted, "Not as though I . . . were already perfect. . . ." Rather, *perfect* means "completely furnished, full-grown, mature." Until the end of his life Paul was pressing forward and growing in the likeness of Jesus Christ.

Bear His Image

Our aim then is to bear the image of Christ. Christ came bearing the Father's image. And "as he is, so are we in this world" (1 John 4:17).

People criticized Jesus. They claimed He desecrated the Sabbath by healing the sick. But they remained silent when He asked, "Which of you convinceth me of sin?"

Everyone knew Christ was different—loving, compassionate, concerned. People said, "Never man spake like this man." And the Greeks voiced the desire of thousands: "We would see Jesus."

Sinners criticize and persecute believers. But admit it or not, they entertain a grudging admiration for the believer who is different, who bucks the trend of the times and follows in the steps of Christ. Sinners haven't changed in the past 2,000 years. They would still see Jesus. And we must bear His image before them.

An image is a resemblance, a reflection of something. Make it as perfect as you will, it can never be completely identical to the real thing. But it serves to remind one of the reality.

The Reverend Flem Van Meter, now deceased, was affectionately called "Daddy" Van Meter by thousands in the Pennsylvania Bible belt. One man expressed the feelings of many in saying, "When I see 'Daddy' Van Meter, I think of Jesus."

This grand old saint loved his Lord supremely. Love conformed him to the image of Christ and he showed it in his Christian walk.

God help us to so love the Lord, to so abide in Him that we bear His image and that others in their minds associate us with the Lord Jesus.

Cultivate Hunger

Jesus often referred to himself as the Son of Man. He "made himself of no reputation . . . and was made in the likeness of men" and "was in all points tempted like as we are, yet without sin" (Philippians 2:7; Hebrews 4:15). So our aim is to be conformed to the image of the Man Christ Jesus. And our help comes from the Son of God, our faithful Intercessor who is seated at the right hand of His Father in heaven.

Jesus was wholly dedicated to the will of the Father. His revelation to Paul on the Damascus road convinced the persecutor that he owed God his complete dedication. He asked, "Lord, what wilt thou have me to do?" (Acts 9:6). This must be the starting point in the life of every soul winner.

Jesus was so dedicated to the will of the Father that He "must needs" go through Samaria. In ministering to one sinful woman He testified: "My meat is to do the will of him that sent me, and to finish his work" (John 4:34).

Children get so wrapped up in their play that meal-time passes unnoticed. Hours later they feel the pangs of hunger. But when they should have been at home eating, their "meat" was making mud pies or playing basketball or football.

What man hasn't been so occupied that he did not crave food? Working on the car. Playing golf—it was an exceptional round. He finally finished in the seventies! Unheard of for him!

What woman hasn't been so occupied on a special shopping day that she forgot about food?

All of us can surely remember a special occasion when our "meat" was something other than food. For Jesus, it was seeking the lost. God give us a spiritual hunger that will only be satisfied by winning the lost.

Seek the Same Spirit and Power

God the Father, God the Son, and God the Holy Spirit are One in heaven. They were One on earth, for the Son of Man was mightily filled with the Holy Spirit before He began His ministry.

The Trinity was revealed at the baptism of Jesus—a Voice, the Son, and a Dove. Led of the Spirit into the wilderness, Jesus later returned in the power of the Spirit to Galilee. There He read from the prophet Isaiah: "The Spirit of the Lord is upon me, because . . . he hath sent me to heal the brokenhearted, to preach deliverance to the captives, and recovering of sight to the blind, to set at liberty them that are bruised . . ." (Luke 4:18).

The Son of Man looked upon the multitudes. He was moved with compassion for them because they were as sheep without a shepherd. He saw man's desperate plight and ministered to the need.

Christ, the Good Shepherd, counted himself expendable for His sheep. A kernel of wheat falls into the ground and dies that it might bring forth more fruit. So He died to bring many sons to glory.

As the ministry of the Son of Man began with the infilling of the Holy Spirit, so must it be for everyone who would bear His image. Man can pity and do nothing. It is the Holy Spirit who sheds the love of God abroad in our hearts (Romans 5:5). And this God-given love causes us to be moved with compassion and to die to selfish interests that we may bring forth more fruit by bringing others to Christ.

After Dwight L. Moody experienced the initial infilling of the Holy Spirit, he said: "My sermons were no different. I did not present any new truths, and yet hundreds were converted." Thoughtfully, he continued: "God has a great many children who do not have the gift of the Holy Ghost for service."

Christ promised His disciples and us the same Spirit and power He had. Only as we claim His promise can we bear His image.

Vessels Unto Honor

What we reflect outwardly of the image of Christ must first be formed in our hearts by the Holy Spirit. For "out of the abundance of the heart the mouth speaketh. . . . Out of [the heart] are the issues of life" (Matthew 12:34; Proverbs 4:23). All we are, all we say, and all we do comes from our heart.

Every Christian is of the earth, earthy. Just a bit of clay, without the Holy Spirit. The prophet said: "O Lord, . . . we are the clay, and thou our potter; and we all are the work of thy hand" (Isaiah 64:8). God likens us to earthen vessels that dispense life to others.

A Minnesota doctor was once unhappy, dejected, short-tempered, and confused—by his own admission. He worked around-the-clock, overdoing everything like a madman to keep his mind occupied and free from conflicts.

"But Christ knocked at my heart and I let Him in. Now I live in a different world; the storm and conflict still rage, the world is still mad, but I have a refuge in Jesus," he says.

Filled with the Spirit, he sincerely recommends the healing virtue of Jesus to his patients. Before performing surgery he turns to God in prayer—a reassurance to many of them.

Now citizens of the community see "Doc" as kindly, unassuming—a true Christian. The consecrated, separated life of service he leads began when he yielded to the Master Potter.

God has chosen and cleansed us. He has shined the light and treasures of the gospel into our hearts. As we yield to Him, the Holy Spirit fashions us into vessels unto honor and meet for the Master's use. The Lord inspires us to pour out unto others the treasures of the Spirit and the Word that we enjoy.

All we are or ever will be for good, we owe to the Master Potter. "It is he that hath made us, and not we ourselves" (Psalm 100:3). So the power and the glory belong to Him alone.

Worth Your Salt

Jesus said: "Ye are the salt of the earth" (Matthew 5:13). He expects every soul winner to serve the same purpose in His program that salt does in natural life.

Salt creates thirst. We need the qualities Jesus enumerated in previous verses—to be poor in spirit, meek, merciful, and pure in heart. Then the people we contact will want to drink from the wells of salvation too. The prophet wrote: "With joy shall ye draw water out of the wells of salvation" (Isaiah 12:3). And Jesus said: "If any man thirst, let him come unto me, and drink" (John 7:37).

22

Salt melts ice. The hearts of many are cold and hard, either from sin or from the vicissitudes of life. Love, mercy, and compassion can melt the coldest and hardest.

A depressed man said, "I'm going to end it all."

Immediately a Christian friend threw an arm around his shoulders and said, "Oh no, you're not."

Love and concern had their effect. The man lives today. He has a reason for living—in Christ.

Salt flavors. Even cakes and pies taste flat if no salt is added. Some people who ridicule the believer would be disappointed if he stumbled and fell. For the child of God shows them there is a better life than their own boring, tasteless existence.

Included in a Roman soldier's pay was an amount to buy his own salt. From this custom came the expression "He's worth his salt." In fact, the word *salary* is derived from the Latin term for salt. God grant that in eternity we will receive pay—or rather, reward—for the effect we have had on the hearts and lives of others.

Let It Shine

Jesus said: "As long as I am in the world, I am the light of the world" (John 9:5). He also said: "Ye are the light of the world" (Matthew 5:14). Sinners need light—guidance to Him who is the Source of divine light and life.

We turn on lights for guidance; to keep from stumbling and falling. Sinners need fall no longer. They can find the good and right way because we are traveling that way.

A young sinner's mother introduced him to a Christian. The youth was wary, prepared to cut the newcomer off at the first mention of religion. Evidently the godly man sensed this, and their conversation

23

revolved around fishing. In fact, during the following months they went fishing together several times.

Then the youth was seriously injured. In the hospital he had plenty of time to think. Who led him to Christ? The fellow fisherman who let his light shine during pleasant hours of conversation and fellowship.

Liberty and freedom have been almost totally eclipsed in communist countries. But even there the light of freedom shines in the embassies of democratic nations. Ambassadors are free men acting in accordance with the will of the nation they represent.

We are citizens of a heavenly country. In this world we represent Christ before men. "Now then we are ambassadors for Christ, as though God did beseech you by us: we pray you in Christ's stead, be ye reconciled to God" (2 Corinthians 5:20). Men who heed this entreaty receive abundant light and eternal life.

The earthly father is overjoyed to see his likeness in the face of his infant son. And God is pleased when He sees the attributes of His Son in us.

3

All This and Eternity Too

Life to the Nth Degree

In Jesus' time the life expectancy was 22 years.
In the Middle Ages it was 33.
In the United States in 1900 it was nearly 50.
Today it is 70 years and reaching beyond.

To whatever combination of factors we ascribe this increase in longevity—education, improved environment, research, medicine—it constitutes an amazing achievement for mankind.

But when we consider what the soul winner has to offer, it is infinitesimal. For under God we are privileged to offer sinful men life to the nth degree. Not 70 years but 70 years multiplied endlessly. We offer life without sin, sickness, and sorrow—eternal, everlasting life.

In John 3:16, Jesus promised everlasting life to all who believe in Him. He further said: "I am come that they might have life, and that they might have it more abundantly. . . . And I give unto them eternal life; and they shall never perish, neither shall any man pluck them out of my hand" (10:10, 28).

Sure, sinners are saved from death and eternal damnation, but this is the negative aspect. It is the by-product of the gift of eternal life. Jesus emphasized the positive when He said: "For God sent not his Son into the world to condemn the world; but that the world through him might be saved" (John 3:17).

What a promise to the worldly man who dreads death, the end of aspiration and hope! Solomon voiced his viewpoint: "All is vanity and vexation of spirit. Yea, I hated all my labor which I had taken under the sun: because I should leave it unto the man that shall be after me" (Ecclesiastes 2:17, 18).

The worldly, sinful man leaves this life sorrowful and empty-handed. But for the believer mortality is swallowed up of life, and he enjoys eternal life, eternal reward, and eternal joy. Eternal life is the soul winner's chief commodity.

Comprehending the Incomprehensible

A man had never believed in the existence of God. To him, God and Santa Claus were buried together. But one night he turned on the TV and listened to a sermon in its entirety. This was a first for him. When the appeal was made, chills raced up and down his spine. Suddenly he knew there was an eternal God. He wanted Him forever and he yielded his life to Him.

However, it is difficult even for the Christian to comprehend eternal life. Salvation from sin, if anything, serves to increase his wonder.

One night the Psalmist cupped his hands around his eyes and stared directly into the heavens. Staggered at the immensity of God and His creation, he cried: "What is man, that thou art mindful of him? and the son of man, that thou visitest him?" (Psalm 8:4).

Christ's disciples were dull of understanding. In fact, some of them departed from Him when He said: "He that believeth on me hath everlasting life. I am that bread of life. . . . He that eateth of this bread shall live for ever. . . . It is the Spirit that quickeneth; the flesh profiteth nothing: the words that I speak unto you, they are spirit, and they are life" (John 6:47, 48, 58, 63).

But Peter, speaking for the Twelve, said: "Lord, to whom shall we go? thou hast the words of eternal life" (v. 68).

When we are saved, we enter another dimension wherein the Holy Spirit is all and in all. And we "are kept by the power of God through faith unto salvation ready to be revealed in the last time" (1 Peter 1:5). Nobody and nothing can separate us from the love of Christ.

In this new dimension, in the realm of the Spirit, eternal realities are spiritually discerned. "Eye hath not seen, nor ear heard, neither have entered into the heart of man, the things which God hath prepared for them that love him. But God hath revealed them unto us by his Spirit" (1 Corinthians 2:9, 10).

Only through the revelation of the Holy Spirit do we begin to grasp the tremendous promise and reality of eternal life.

Invisible in Time

Eternal life and the things related to it are invisible. But does this make it less believable and real?

Dr. Wernher von Braun believes many people today feel that science has somehow made religious ideas untimely or old-fashioned.

"But science has a real surprise for skeptics," he says in the tract "The Farther We Probe Into Space, the Greater My Faith" (Springfield, MO: Assemblies of God, 1966). "Science tells us that nothing in nature, not even the tiniest particle, can disappear without a trace."

"Now if God applies this fundamental principle to the most minute and insignificant parts of His universe, doesn't it make sense to assume that He applies it also to the masterpiece of His creation—man and his soul? . . . Everything science has taught me—and continues to teach me—strengthens my belief in the continuity of our spiritual existence after death. Nothing disappears without a trace.''

The apostle Paul saw a close parallel between the natural and the spiritual, between the finite and the infinite. He wrote: "The things which are seen are temporal; but the things which are not seen are eternal" (2 Corinthians 4:18). "His invisible attributes, that is to say his everlasting power and deity, have been visible, ever since the world began, to the eye of reason, in the things he has made" (Romans 1:20, NEB).

Life is seeing. "For now [in this life] we see through a glass, darkly, but then [in the life to come] face to face" (1 Corinthians 13:12). Temporal things are but a shadow of eternal realities.

Life is knowing. "Now [in this life] I know in part; but then [in the life to come] shall I know even as also I am known" (1 Corinthians 13:12). Now "all things are naked and opened unto the eyes of him with whom we have to do" (Hebrews 4:13). In the life to come, He will impart this knowledge unto us.

Life is doing. Death is the cessation of all activity. Eternal life will be occupied with unwearying, joyful activity. Christ has promised eternal spheres of influence and responsibility to those who hear His "Well done . . ." (Matthew 25:21).

Fellowship Forever

The only way the eternal God can grant the gift of eternal life is to adopt us into His family. To make us partakers of His divine nature.

What a transformation occurs when we are born again from above! Reborn to fellowship with God.

This is a close-knit relationship and family. John the Beloved said: "Truly our fellowship is with the Father, and with his Son Jesus Christ" (1 John 1:3). God delights to fellowship with His sons. As for us, the Psalmist put it: "In thy presence is fullness of joy; at thy right hand there are pleasures for evermore" (Psalm 16:11).

Once we attended church. We supported it halfheartedly and did commendable things—when it suited us. But having never repented of our sins, we were outside the family of God—aliens. We could expect no divine revelations and gifts.

But since we are children of God, it follows that we are also "heirs of God, and joint-heirs with Christ" (Romans 8:17).

Rev. C. M. Ward told the story of the godly newsman, Royal Brougham. In 1909, Portus Baxter hired him as a cub reporter. Years passed and Brougham became nationally known as an outstanding sports editor, while retirement crept up on Baxter.

After the death of Baxter's wife, Brougham kept the lonely old gentleman on the payroll for a token amount to make him feel he still belonged. And he provided his elderly friend with credentials and a press pass for important events.

At 95, Portus Baxter died. He left his entire fortune—$400,000 in top securities—to his longtime friend. Brougham talked to God about his inheritance and then put the money in trust "to help needy youth attend Christian-related schools."

Baxter made Brougham his heir because Brougham chose to befriend him and to fellowship with him. God makes us His heirs because we choose Him instead of the pleasures of sin for a season. So we have "an inheritance [which is] incorruptible, and undefiled, and that fadeth not away, reserved in heaven for [us]" (1 Peter 1:4).

Satan, the accuser of the brethren, once tried to convince God that Job was unworthy to fellowship with Him and that he served God for what he got out of it.

Satan can well make the same point about every one of us. "What right have they to eternal life? They are unworthy," he can say.

It's true. Every Christian is silenced by this accusation—well aware of his unworthiness.

When Aleksandr Solzhenitsyn visited the United States in 1975, he told about his imprisonment in Russia. One of the hardest things to endure was the silence imposed upon him by his jailors. Prisoners were forbidden to speak.

A fellow prisoner noticed the effect upon Solzhenitsyn. With each succeeding day he became weaker and more depressed. Finally, without saying a word, this man took a stick and drew a cross in the dust.

Solzhenitsyn looked. Immediately, he remembered his destiny. Because of the tremendous price his Triune God had paid at Calvary, he had everlasting life and an eternal inheritance. The silence between his soul and God was broken. Imprisonment could not separate him "from the love of God, which is in Christ Jesus" (Romans 8:39).

There's an answer to the accuser of the brethren— the Cross. And the eternal Word of God breaks the silence for man saying, "Worthy is the Lamb that was slain . . ." (Revelation 5:12).

We become worthy of salvation and eternal life by virtue of our faith in Christ's atoning death. The Possessor of heaven and earth became a pauper and died in our stead. The divine logic of it all is contained in Romans 8:32-34: "He that spared not his own Son, but delivered him up for us all, how shall he not with him also freely give us all things? Who shall lay any thing to the charge of God's elect? It is God that justifieth. . . . It is Christ that died . . . who also maketh intercession for us.''

Eternal Life Displayed

Reason and logic sometimes fail to convince men of the worth of something offered to them. Instead, many are swayed by their senses. The world and Satan capitalize on this fact.

Children watch TV bug-eyed as animated toys go through interesting gyrations. What a let-down when they handle the toy and learn it takes patience and perseverance to operate the gadget! And then what appeared to take minutes on TV is over in seconds.

Satan-inspired men produce cheap, tawdry movies and spend millions showing sensual excerpts on TV. Gullible viewers flock to local drive-ins while the producers rake in more millions—laughing all the way from the box office to the bank.

On the other hand, food processors promote a good product by making eye-appealing displays in supermarkets. They throw in the clincher by offering bite-size samples to shoppers. Sight and taste persuade many to buy what they otherwise would idly pass by.

What sold us on eternal life? What convinced us of the reality of the invisible? God made us and He knows us. So He manifested eternal life. He displayed it in His eternal Son:

Author of life—''I am the life.''

Master of death—''I am the resurrection.''

Conqueror of demons—''He cast out many devils.''

Ruler of the forces of nature—''Peace, be still.''

John the Beloved concluded: ''That which was from the beginning, which we have heard, which we have seen with our eyes, which we have looked upon, and our hands have handled, of the Word of life; (for the life was manifested, and we have seen it, and bear witness, and show unto you that eternal life, which was with the Father, and was manifested unto us;) that which we have seen and heard declare we unto you" (1 John 1:1-3).

The apostles displayed eternal life in Christ to their generation by their lives and ministries. Multitudes "took knowledge of them, that they had been with Jesus" (Acts 4:13), and they too became heirs of an eternal inheritance.

We display the assurance of eternal life in word and deed by manifesting "love, joy, peace, long-suffering, gentleness, goodness, faith, meekness, temperance" in our daily lives (Galatians 5:22, 23). Showing our generation that there is no disappointment in Jesus.

Accepting the Gift

Even in apostolic days men tried to gain eternal life by natural means. The rich young ruler asked: "What good thing shall I do?" (Matthew 19:16). The Bible replies: "Not of works, lest any man should boast" (Ephesians 2:9).

Simon the sorcerer "thought that the gift of God may be purchased with money" (Acts 8:20). Peter rebuked him and even all today who try by charity and good deeds to inherit eternal life. For it is a gift—"The gift of God is eternal life" (Romans 6:23).

A San Francisco mounted policeman escorted children across the street at their school for 14 years. Then while chasing three thieves in Golden Gate Park, he fell from his horse. The concussion left him unconscious for 2 weeks.

While recuperating one warm summer day on his front porch, he looked up to see more than 50 children approaching. "Hi, Mr. Ed!" the youngsters, aged 5 to 12, chorused. They sang "For He's a Jolly Good

Fellow'' and presented him with a portable television set purchased with pennies they had saved.

How did he react to this loving gift? Offer to reimburse the children? Of course not. That would have broken their hearts.

As the children sang, the patrolman wept. Then he smiled from ear to ear and thanked them.

How should man react to the offer of eternal life? Realizing the love of God and his own unworthiness, he repents of the sin that separates him from the Lord. Many times penitential tears flow.

Knowing eternal life is a gift of divine love, he believes the Lord Jesus intends it for him. He believes and accepts it just as simply as the patrolman received the childrens' gift. Every day he rejoices in the reality of everlasting life and worships God who gave it.

Men do not discard valuable earthly possessions just because they are gifts. Rather, they cherish gifts of love more than things they have purchased. So it must be with eternal life.

The apostle Paul charged Timothy to "fight the good fight of faith, lay hold on eternal life, whereunto thou art also called, and hast professed a good profession before many witnesses" (1 Timothy 6:12).

As possessors of eternal life, we are engaged in a spiritual work and warfare. Let us occupy until Christ returns.

4
Tools to Transform

God Kept His Word for Us

How do we know we have eternal life? Because we feel good? Not necessarily. Because we have met the conditions spelled out in the Word of God? Yes.

The foundation of Christian beliefs and experiences is the Bible. John the Beloved wrote: "These things have I written unto you . . . that ye may know that ye have eternal life" (1 John 5:13).

Had we no Bible, we would be warriors without a weapon, builders without a tool, teachers without a textbook. The Bible is an essential in Christian life and testimony. Its preservation for us is a miracle.

God inspired scores of men to write the Bible. He inspired—and continues to inspire—people to translate it into many languages. Not to be outdone, the devil has moved men to destroy the written Word.

In 1524, some 87 years before the King James Version of the Bible was printed, God inspired William Tyndale to translate the Scriptures into the language of the common people. Rebuffed in his efforts to have it printed in England, Tyndale went to Germany. A year later friendly London merchants financed this venture and began to smuggle his New Testaments into England in bales of merchandise.

Cuthbert Tunstall, Bishop of London, got wind of this and ordered all copies to be confiscated and burned.

His embargo was so successful that lack of funds was about to force Tyndale to quit.

Unaware of his success, Bishop Tunstall endeavored to cut off the smuggling operation at its source. He asked Augustine Pakington, a London merchant trading in Antwerp, if he could arrange to buy up everything Tyndale printed. A secret friend of Tyndale and a smuggler himself, Pakington agreed cautiously to try.

Profits from Bishop Tunstall's purchases enabled Tyndale to expand his printing operations. And within 3 months Pakington and other merchants were smuggling three times as many New Testaments into England through other channels. The bishop was outfoxed.

Many risked their lives to preserve the Bible for us. In fact, Tyndale made the supreme sacrifice. In 1536, he was captured and burned at the stake.

Most Powerful Tool

The Bible is still the world's best-seller. Millions have it in their homes. But too often it gathers dust and serves as a repository for old recipes, that "lucky" four-leaf clover, or the letter one wants to keep. As such, it is a tool on the shelf. It accomplishes nothing without a worker to wield it.

A godly pastor once said: "The help a minister gives will not be a bed to lie on—it will be a sword to fight with." And he could well have added: A hammer to break the rock in pieces (Jeremiah 23:29) or an awl to prick the guilty conscience. Pastors, teachers, and soul winners use what God gives them. And their most effective tool is the Spirit-breathed Word of God.

The Scriptures are more important than the soul winner, his reasonings, and his logic. Besides, a witness may be adversely affected by his own trials. He may forget to depend on the guidance and help of the Holy Spirit. So he may fail to impress sinners for God.

But God's Word is forever settled in heaven. It is positive, pungent, and powerful. It "shall not pass away" (Matthew 24:35).

What a soul winner says may be soon forgotten. But the Biblical quote unfailingly registers in the mind and soul of the sinful hearer. The witness may be long gone, but the Holy Spirit has total recall. He can bring that living Word back forcefully to the mind of the unbeliever again and again. And He surely will if the witness adds continuing prayer to his testimony.

A Christian soldier knew all this. When his company received word that they would attack in the morning, a number of replacements asked for a New Testament. Combat was a new and fearful thing.

Unable to find the chaplain, the godly GI spent several hours that night scrounging up New Testaments and Gospel portions for his buddies.

Who could tell what had prompted their desire for God's Word? The prayers of parents? The remembrance of family worship, Sunday school, a once-memorized Scripture verse? It was important to get God's Word into their hands. For 2 days later, 50 percent of the company were casualties.

Knowledge That Changes

Intelligent, fluent, neat, kind—these adjectives have been used to describe effective witnesses. But one man who won many to Christ failed to finish the fifth grade. Others have influenced men for Christ on the job; at work that made them dirty—not neat.

An extremely important attribute of a soul winner is a knowledge of the Bible. It is necessary to memorize key Scripture verses; to have them at tongue-tip. But an understanding of the Word of God is of even greater value.

Jesus said: "If ye abide in me, and my words abide in you, ye shall ask what ye will, and it shall be done unto you. Herein is my Father glorified, that ye bear much fruit" (John 15:7, 8).

Fruitful witnesses read the Bible prayerfully daily, again and again. The Holy Spirit enlightens the understanding, filling us "with the knowledge of his will in all wisdom and spiritual understanding; that ye might walk worthy of the Lord unto all pleasing, being fruitful in every good work, and increasing in the knowledge of God" (Colossians 1:9, 10).

A Sunday school teacher realized that Calvary had become a familiar, oft-repeated story. It had ceased to stir his emotions, to enliven his teaching and testimony.

So he began to read the Crucifixion story every morning: Monday, in Matthew; Tuesday, Mark; Wednesday, Luke; Thursday, John; and Friday, back to Matthew. A month passed. Then one morning as he was reading, he received a fresh revelation of the love of Christ. Tears welled up in his eyes. Falling to his knees, he poured out his soul in love and adoration to the Saviour who had first loved him, who gave His all and died in his stead.

Never again could he tell the story of Calvary without emotion. His students saw it stirred his soul. One after another they accepted Christ as their Saviour and Lord.

Reading the Bible changes us and increases our knowledge of God and His great plan of redemption.

How to Believe

God's Word generates faith.

Faith is not a will-o'-the-wisp, ethereal something— now you have it, now you don't. Faith has a firm foundation in fact.

37

We believe George Washington was the "father" of our country. True, we never saw him. So what is the basis of our faith? The writings of many historians.

The apostle Paul wrote: "For whosoever shall call upon the name of the Lord shall be saved. . . . [Saving] faith cometh by hearing, and hearing by the word of God" (Romans 10:13, 17).

Faith awakens in the heart of the sinner upon hearing the message or testimony about a loving God who forgives the repentant. And the message itself comes through or is based on the Word of God.

That living Word was written by 40 Spirit-inspired men over a period of about 1,600 years. Nevertheless, they agree—giving the same unvarying testimony about our Triune God; a God who loves His creatures. He tenderly calls to erring men: "All day long I have stretched forth my hands unto a disobedient and gainsaying people" (Romans 10:21); and, "Come unto me, all ye that labor and are heavy laden, and I will give you rest" (Matthew 11:28).

A Christian was unable to persuade a man to accept Christ's invitation. But before concluding the conversation, he gave the sinner a New Testament. The recipient promised to read it.

In church several weeks later, the witness heard a man testify: "I have accepted Jesus as my Saviour." Holding up a New Testament, he continued: "About a month ago, a man gave this to me. It led me to Jesus."

So the soul winner and the former unbeliever met again, because of the power of the Scriptures.

Witnesses do not generate faith. The Word of God does. It accomplishes what no man can do. It continues to work when the most dedicated soul winner fails to convince another to accept Christ.

When Jesus was being tried by Pilate, many people cried, "Let him be crucified." They consented unto the death of Him who had done only good. Later, they heard He had risen from the dead. And they were probably told that Jesus' disciples had stolen His body.

Life resumed its normal routine. Weeks passed. The trial and crucifixion of Jesus was only a memory that troubled them infrequently. But the Day of Pentecost arrived, and they heard strange stories of events at the temple.

They hurried to the site and eventually heard Peter, whom they recognized as a disciple of Jesus. With the Scriptures he probed the deepest recesses of their souls. They were sinners, murderers, and they knew it. Now they also knew "the heart is deceitful above all things, and desperately wicked" (Jeremiah 17:9). And they cried, "Men and brethren, what shall we do?" (Acts 2:37).

Having used the Word for diagnosis, Peter was now prepared with the scriptural remedy—repentance and forgiveness of sins. His audience was not ignorant of the divine plan. It was written in the Law, the Psalms,and the Prophets. How many times they had chanted the confession of David in Psalm 51!

Modern sinners must be convinced of their true condition in the sight of God. They must know the way to escape. That knowledge must come from the Bible.

Standing outside his church, a 12-year-old was inviting people to enter. As a woman walked by, he said, "What you need, you can find here."

The woman stopped and looked at the youth thoughtfully. Then she slowly entered the church. She heard the gospel message and it changed her life and destiny. Afterward she told the pastor the boy had interrupted her plan to commit suicide. The boy knew that the diagnosis and cure for the sin-sick soul was where the Word was proclaimed.

Rightly Using the Word

The Word of God must be used properly. Tools wrongly used can make them ineffective for their designed application. If a woodsaw is used to cut metal, soon it will not cut even wood.

Have you ever tried to saw a board square and straight? It takes skill. Skill comes from study, training, and practice. Carpenters aren't born; they are made.

The apostle Paul advised young Timothy: "Study to show thyself approved unto God, a workman that needeth not to be ashamed, rightly dividing the word of truth" (2 Timothy 2:15). Soul winners aren't born; they are trained.

When one handles a circular saw, revolving at 5,000 revolutions a minute, he must rightly use it. After cutting through a piece of plywood, a man unthinkingly lowered his arm. Somehow, the still-revolving blade bit into his leg, into the bone. He was in the hospital for several weeks. Prompt action by skilled surgeons saved his leg.

"The word of God is quick, and powerful, and sharper than any two-edged sword, piercing even to the dividing asunder of soul and spirit, and of the joints and marrow, and is a discerner of the thoughts and intents of the heart" (Hebrews 4:12).

Tools designed to accomplish a specific task quickly and well can be ineffective or even destructive in the hands of an unskilled workman. This applies to the witness and the Word. The Bible is rightly used to lay bare the evil thoughts and intents of human hearts. To stop there is to be unskilled in its use.

Jesus was a master at convincing men of their sins. But before He spoke of perishing, He said: "For God so loved the world, that he gave his only begotten Son . . ." (John 3:16). To be approved unto God in the use of His Word, the soul winner must present not only the cause but also the cure, not only the sickness but also the remedy, not only the sin but also the Saviour.

The Personal Touch

Properly used, the soul winner's personal encounter with Jesus is a tool of inestimable value. Humbly and sincerely told, it shows that salvation is real, not theoretical; understandable, not vague; and provided by a living Saviour, not a benign influence.

The woman of Samaria met Jesus at Jacob's Well. Transformed by this encounter, she hurried into Sychar and excitedly cried to all who would listen: "Come, see a man, which told me all things that ever I did: is not this the Christ?" (4:29).

No doubt this personal experience and testimony provoked varied reactions:

"What wound her up?"

"I've always snubbed her. What made her speak to me?"

"Told her all that she ever did? Why wouldn't she play this down?"

Nevertheless, it was evident there was a marked change in the woman. Changed by the Christ? They just had to check this out.

The Samaritan woman's testimony bore fruit. Many people of her city believed on Jesus and said to her: "Now we believe, not because of thy saying: for we have heard him ourselves, and know that this is indeed the Christ, the Saviour of the world" (v. 42).

One whole town despised a certain man. Even members of the church Ben's mother attended could hardly stomach him. His primary contacts with them were arrests for disturbing the services when he was drunk.

But in a drunken stupor one night he either fell repeatedly or was severely beaten. When he sobered up the following morning, he was unable to get out of bed. Suffering from broken ribs and bruises over most of his body, he cried out to God for help and mercy. Christ heard him and saved him.

Immediately, Ben began to testify to all who would listen that he had met God. People soon began to acknowledge that such a transformation could have come only through Christ. Now they refer people with delirium tremens and drug addiction to Ben and his church. He simply recounts what Christ did for him.

Love Never Faileth

"The love of Christ constraineth" the soul winner to seek the lost (2 Corinthians 5:14). Realizing, then, that he is moving in the divine will, he believes the Holy Spirit is present to convict the sinner.

The apostle Paul knew this and promised the Philippian jailer: "Believe on the Lord Jesus Christ, and thou shalt be saved, and thy house" (Acts 16:31). "You see that faith co-operated with his good deeds, and by his good deeds faith was made complete" (James 2:22, Williams). The jailer and his family believed and rejoiced in the Lord.

This happened too because Paul held no animosity in his heart for the man who made his feet fast in the stocks. Paul loved him and prevented him from committing suicide. The love of Christ in the apostle's heart had great effect on the jailer. Later, Paul wrote: "Charity never faileth. . . . And now abideth faith, hope, charity [love], these three; but the greatest of these is charity" (1 Corinthians 13:8, 13).

During a thunderstorm a little girl threw herself into her mother's arms crying, "I'm afraid!"

The mother tried to quiet the child by reminding her of God's loving and protecting care. But the little one clung the closer. "I know God loves me, Mommy," she said, "but when it's thundering and lightning, I want someone with skin on to love me!"

This is one of the reasons Jesus took on human form. This is the reason angels do not proclaim the gospel message. Sinful men need "someone with skin on to love" them. And Jesus commands us: "Thou shalt love thy neighbor as thyself" (Matthew 19:19).

Everyone has a dire need for love. Psychiatrist A. A. Brill once wrote: "It is quite as essential for a person to have love as to have pure air and food to sustain him."

The witness needs the tools of the Word, experience, and faith. But love is the combination wrench. Using it in conjunction with the others, the soul winner, under God, accomplishes his task and wins souls for Jesus Christ.

5
Laws of the Harvest

Sticking and Broadcasting

"If there's a harvest ahead, even a distant one, it is poor thrift to be stingy of your seed." So wrote Thomas Carlyle.

In the spring the gardener painstakingly sticks seed onions into prepared soil. He simply presses them into the ground. Harvest can begin in 6 to 8 weeks. Fresh spring onions will be on the table.

To sow wheat in like manner would be a never-ending task. Drill or "broadcast" sowing equipment is used. Although it is more distant, a harvest is expected. God sends sun and rain and gives the increase.

In "sticking" onions the sower avoids hard, rocky soil. He knows every good seed will produce a harvest. But the farmer cannot be a chooser in planting wheat. Knowing that some will fall on rocky ground or in shallow soil, he must not be stingy with the seed. The wise farmer sows bountifully in order to receive a bountiful harvest.

There is a spiritual harvest ahead. Jesus said of it: "The harvest is the end of the world [age]" (Matthew 13:39). Then He will return for all the redeemed.

Sure, the skeptics say: "Where is the promise of his coming? . . . all things continue as they were from the beginning of the creation" (2 Peter 3:4). But the laws of the harvest are unalterable. When natural seeds are planted, they yield a harvest. And when a soul winner plants good seed in human hearts, he should expect a harvest.

Sometimes the weather turns damp and cold and the seed lies dormant in the ground. But no gardener or farmer pokes around seed he has planted to see if it is germinating. He realizes this condition is beyond his control.

Gospel seed may lie dormant in the human heart for years. The soul winner has no control over it. He is simply responsible to faithfully plant and water. God is responsible for the increase.

Known Only to God

"In this bright little package, now isn't it odd?
You've a dime's worth of something known only to God!"

—Edgar A. Guest

Kept in a colorful little packet, a seed remains dry and dormant. True, it contains the germ of life given by the Creator. But Jesus said: "Except a corn of wheat fall into the ground and die, it abideth alone: but if it die, it bringeth forth much fruit" (John 12:24). God cannot transform it into a beautiful, living plant and it cannot produce a harvest while it's in the packet.

Seed dies and comes to life only after someone plants it. This is true naturally and spiritually. Angels do not plant the seed of God's Word. Neither does the Holy Spirit, apart from human agency. Sowing is man's responsibility and duty.

Sowing begins in the home and extends into every area the soul winner reaches—to the ends of the earth perhaps. The prophet put it: "Blessed are ye that sow beside all waters" (Isaiah 32:20). Scatter precious seed freely and widely. Sow in every type of soil.

With his mother and sister a young boy sowed the

seed in his home. His father and his brother came to Christ. He scattered the seed in street meetings with others from his church. The public address system carried the seed into a third-floor apartment across the street. An invalid Jewish man listened behind drawn shades. He called upon his Messiah and died a Christian.

Then the young man married a godly girl, and they sowed the seed in their home, in life and in family worship. Their son became a Christian.

Years passed and God led this man into the ministry of writing. He reached even into the mission field, to the ends of the earth.

Known only to God is the process that takes a dormant seed through death into abundant life. Known only to God are the possibilities that abide in the life of him who determines to be a sower, a soul winner.

Consistency Pays Off

The apostle wrote: "The husbandman waiteth for the precious fruit of the earth, and hath long patience for it, until he receive the early and latter rain" (James 5:7). "By patient continuance in well doing" (Romans 2:7), by consistently sowing and depending on God, the sower reaps a harvest.

Spiritual sowing has its similarities. The soul winner must not become discouraged by lack of results from a single planting. If one person isn't moved, the next individual may heed the message. And the fact that a sinner turns him off is no indication he will do so the second, third, fourth. . . time the seed is sown.

Two men worked in a shop for over 8 years. The Christian consistently witnessed to his friend. But it seemed he was broadcasting seed on hard, rocky soil.

The believer knew a beautiful, little daughter had come into the home and heart of the sinner. Almost 3 years later, the father was talking about her upcoming birthday and his plans for the occasion when suddenly, it occurred to the witness that here was prepared, broken ground. So he simply stuck a seed into the yielding soil. He asked what happened in Sunday school on a child's birthday.

"Oh, she doesn't go to Sunday school," the unbelieving father said.

"But Jesus said: 'Suffer the little children to come unto me, and forbid them not; for of such is the kingdom of God.' Little ones enjoy the story of Jesus and His love. They have no great sins to confess. They soon invite Him into their hearts. But you are keeping your child from learning to love Jesus."

The soul winner paused and looked into the eyes of his now dead-serious fellow employee. "Please take your little girl to Sunday school. You owe it to her."

That seed took root. The child was in Sunday school the following Sunday. And there was a harvest. The following week father and mother accepted Christ.

Don't Change Seed

The sower may have the necessary know-how. He may have the latest and best in sowing equipment. He may also be patient and consistent. The end result can still be frustrating and unsatisfactory.

A man planted grass seed around his new home. The weather turned hot and dry. Despite frequent sprinkling, many bare spots dotted the lawn. He had planted good, tested seed and had exceeded the supplier's recommendations on the amount of seed to be sown. He was not frustrated. Not yet.

Believing there was still seed in the lawn that had not germinated and knowing the shorter, cooler days of fall would cause the grass to tiller and spread, he simply followed fertilizing recommendations and waited. In fact, he waited 2 years. Dry years. There were still too many bare spots.

Then he decided to loosen the soil in the bare spots and plant seed. He tried to save money by using a slightly cheaper brand. After all, it contained considerably less than 1 percent weed seeds. The bare spots filled in, and all over his lawn weed seeds germinated—broadleaf fescue. The only way to combat it was to dig it out. Then he was frustrated. He learned to plant only the best seed.

The soul winner's seed is the Word of God. Anything less—opinions and philosophies of men—is not good seed. The apostle was quite dogmatic about this: "Though we, or an angel from heaven, preach any other gospel unto you . . . let him be accursed" (Galatians 1:8).

A believer may go through a spiritual dry spell. Whether it is his witness to an individual or his over-all efforts, he may feel the results are less than satisfactory. Nevertheless, he must not change or adulterate the seed.

The end result of sowing adulterated seed will not "be found unto praise and honor and glory at the appearing of Jesus Christ" (1 Peter 1:7).

Lacks in the Soil

Now the sower may be diligent, patient, and consistent. He may use good, unadulterated seed. But the results still depend in great measure on the soil. Jesus pointed this out in the Parable of the Sower.

The sower and the seed were constants. There was no variation in the sowing process. All the ground was seeded in the same manner. So the results depended on the quality and condition of the soil.

The Lord said some seed fell by the wayside, upon

rocks and among thorns, without result. Only when it fell into good ground did it produce a harvest.

Christ said the wayside hearer is hard. He lacks spiritual desire. Oh, he hears. But perhaps he does not fully understand, and he makes no effort to do so. Then the devil brings something else to his mind, and the truth is forgotten.

Seed sown on rocks represents the individual who does not fully count the cost. He does not make his calling and election sure. He receives the message joyfully "yet hath he not root in himself, but dureth for awhile: for when tribulation or persecution ariseth because of the word, by and by he is offended" (Matthew 13:21). This person lacks determination.

Then seed fell among thorns which illustrate the cares, pleasures, and riches of life. These spring up more quickly and vigorously than the seed and choke it out. The individual represented here lacks room in his heart for Jesus.

Christ looked on the rich young ruler and loved him. But even He couldn't persuade him to choose eternal life rather than worldly pleasure. And Jesus remarked: "How hardly shall they that have riches enter into the kingdom of God!" (Mark 10:23).

The Lord tenderly invites "whosoever." He fulfills all His good promises to wayward men who come to Him. He inspires many to witness to His saving grace. But He will not—and soul winners cannot—compel men to accept His great salvation.

Soil Can Change

Jesus' Parable of the Sower and the Soils was just that—an illustration of the fact that individuals are different. Not all respond to the gospel in the same way. But the Lord did not teach that soil conditions are unchangeable.

49

"Judah shall plow, and Jacob shall break his clods. Sow to yourselves in righteousness, reap in mercy; break up your fallow ground: for it is time to seek the Lord, till he come and rain righteousness upon you" (Hosea 10:11, 12). Hard soil can be broken up.

The parting of the ways came for two teenage friends. One went to Bible school. The other joined the navy. In correspondence the godly youth challenged his buddy to trust Christ for salvation. Replying, the sailor related his indulgences in sin and his narrow escapes from death. Infrequently, he admitted to a hunger for something more satisfying—God perhaps.

Honorably discharged from the navy, the sinner engaged his godly friend in many discussions about a God who is concerned about His creatures. A God who exerts His power to answer the prayer of faith. Gradually, the worldly man's attitude began to change.

Then one day at 2 a.m., the soul winner's phone rang. An excited voice said God had saved him while driving home from a business trip. Suddenly, Jesus had become real, and he accepted His great salvation. It was his longtime friend.

It took 16 years to break up that fallow ground. Then the ex-sailor became an enthusiastic witness for Christ.

Finally, in His parable, Jesus said seed fell into good ground. This pictures those "which in an honest and good heart, having heard the word, keep it, and bring forth fruit with patience" (Luke 8:15). Some obey the Word as soon as they hear it. Others come to Christ only if a soul winner keeps sowing the seed.

No Water—No Harvest

To be seeded, soil needs moisture. In Israel the early rains begin in October. They prepare the ground for plowing and planting. The latter rains begin in February and last through April. They make possible the harvest. We must have rain. No rain—no harvest.

On his second missionary journey the apostle Paul ministered in Corinth. Many heard the gospel for the first time and were converted. Later, Paul wrote: "I have planted, Apollos watered" (1 Corinthians 3:6). Now what was Apollos' special gift?

Apollos was an "eloquent man, and mighty in the Scriptures . . . he . . . helped them much which had believed through grace: for he mightily convinced the Jews, and that publicly, showing by the Scriptures that Jesus was Christ" (Acts 18:24-28). Christ desired to "sanctify and cleanse it [the Church] with the washing of water by the word" (Ephesians 5:26).

So Apollos watered congregations and individuals with the Scriptures. He persuaded people who had heard the gospel—those in the valley of decision—to accept Christ. The faith of some wavered. He helped establish them more firmly upon the Rock. And he helped every Christian to "grow in grace, and in the knowledge of our Lord and Saviour Jesus Christ" (2 Peter 3:18). Apollos watered spiritual soil with the Word and prepared it for the harvest.

How many young converts would have gone back into sin if an established Christian witness had not watered them with the encouraging Word? How many have gone back because everyone assumed they would automatically—somehow—be grounded in the faith?

Many times individuals we convince have long since been pricked in their hearts in family worship, in Sunday school, or by another witness. We just faithfully water their hearts with the Spirit-breathed Word. And the Holy Spirit does His mighty office work.

God's Responsibility

Probably Paul ministered to individuals in Corinth, and (like Jesus with the rich young ruler) he loved them. But he had to depart for other fields of labor leaving them still dead in sin. No doubt Apollos preached to some of the same people without result. They faithfully ministered, the Holy Spirit convicted, and "God gave the increase" (1 Corinthians 3:6).

A fine young couple began attending church. The pastor noticed that Sunday evening after Sunday evening they were under conviction for sin. He spoke to them. He visited in their home without success. Then they absented themselves from church.

The pastor asked a godly grandfather to visit the young couple. He readily agreed to do so. He loved them immediately. They talked about many things— work, parents, future plans. The old gentleman saw they enjoyed his company. Over an hour passed, and he gently turned the conversation to Christ's love for them. Without urging they fell to their knees and accepted Him.

Pastor and parishioner talked about it later. Perhaps the young couple associated the elderly soul winner with home and parents. They couldn't be sure. But this they knew: the pastor sowed, the witness watered, and God alone gave the increase.

God did not intend that Paul, Apollos, or you should save anyone from their sins. Just do your part. Be faithful. Do not become discouraged. God alone is responsible for the increase.

6
Go With the Wind

Jesus called His 12 disciples unto Him and "gave them power" to minister in His name (Matthew 10:1). He gave a mission to the Twelve and then to the Seventy. They returned with joy saying that even the demons were subject unto them.

But with this experience in the ministry, they still needed to wait for the promise of the Father. They were not ready to be witnesses unto Christ until they had been baptized in the Holy Spirit (Acts 1:8).

On May 20, 1927, a young United States airmail pilot was studying weather data and charting storms. He found a miniature cyclone was moving eastward into the Atlantic. Hurrying to his small monoplane, the *Spirit of St. Louis*, he took off from Roosevelt Field, Long Island, flying with the wind.

Thirty-three-and-a-half hours later Charles Lindbergh landed in Paris. The courageous young aviator had made the first transatlantic nonstop solo flight in history. His airplane went faster and further on a limited supply of fuel than it ever could have gone without the help of the wind.

When the Holy Spirit came on the Day of Pentecost, there was "a sound from heaven as of a rushing mighty wind. . . . And they were all filled with the Holy Ghost" (Acts 2:2, 4). They arose from that place of prayer and blessing and went with the wind. Through the power of

53

the Holy Spirit the apostles turned the hearts of sinful multitudes to Christ.

We need to be filled with the Holy Spirit. We need an enduement of power from on high. We need an ever-present Comforter, Helper, and Guide.

Soul winning is a great challenge. It demands our best. And yet our best is not enough. The apostles' best was not enough. They set us an example and proved the promises of Christ. Only through the infilling and enablement of the Holy Spirit can men win others to Christ.

Abundant Spirit

One must receive before he can give. He must be filled before he can pour out.

A pharmacist bought some land on the outskirts of a small community and erected a building. Since the town's water mains did not extend to his lots, he drilled a well. At 75 feet the driller hit a good stream. But several years later the well went dry.

The pharmacist called the well driller again. When he deepened the well to 166 feet, he hit a real bonanza. No matter how much he pumped, the water level remained constant.

Neighbors' wells had gone dry, so the druggist began to supply them. Eventually, he drilled two more wells. With three electric pumps, a 100,000-gallon tank, and 1½ miles of pipe, he was in business. He could help others because he had an abundant supply.

Jesus said: "Whosoever drinketh of the water that I shall give him shall never thirst; but the water that I shall give him shall be in him a well of water springing up into everlasting life" (John 4:14). Thus the longing of the individual is satisfied.

Later Jesus said: "He that believeth on me [drinking living water], as the Scripture hath said, out of his belly [innermost being] shall flow rivers of living water" (7:38). Here's a supply for others. Here's the pouring out, the giving.

But how can this be? How can finite man pour out a divine supply for others? Is not this the divine prerogative?

The writer of the Gospel explained it in John 7:39: "But this spake he of the Spirit, which they that believe on him should receive." So it is "not I but Christ," and the provisions and the enablement He has granted us through the indwelling Spirit. As the apostle said: "I can do all things through Christ which strengtheneth me" (Philippians 4:13).

The Available Spirit

On the Day of Pentecost, Peter was inspired to say: "This Jesus . . . having received of the Father the promise of the Holy Ghost, he hath shed forth this, which ye now see and hear. . . . Repent . . . and ye shall receive the gift of the Holy Ghost. For the promise is unto you, and to your children, and to all that are afar off, even as many as the Lord our God shall call" (Acts 2:32, 33, 38, 39).

In the throng listening to Peter were many who had crucified Jesus. Many who had shouted, "Let Him be crucified." They could well have doubted that the promise could be for them. But they repented and learned the Holy Spirit was available to whosoever.

"They continued steadfastly in the apostles' doctrine and fellowship. . . . And the Lord added to the church daily such as should be saved" (vv. 42, 47). They were living proof to others that the Holy Spirit dwelled in the hearts of believers.

Undoubtedly, members of the Early Church won multitudes to Christ because "they were all filled with the Holy Ghost, and they spake the word of God with boldness'' (4:31).

We are the "afar off" people, and the promised Holy Spirit is available to us. For the eternal God says: "I am the Lord, I change not" (Malachi 3:6).

Evangelist Billy Graham said: "The time has come to give the Holy Spirit His rightful place in our preaching, in our teaching, and in our churches. . . . We need to learn once again what it means to be baptized with the Holy Spirit. . . . We can rationalize and immediately ten thousand theological questions arise and we try to figure it all out; but, brethren, I want to tell you that we need to accept, we need to get something. Give it any terminology you want, but we do not have the same enthusiasm, the same dynamics and the same power the Early Church had. . . . They had the filling of the Holy Spirit.''*

The Holy Spirit makes himself available today. He condescends to work through weak human instruments. How foolish we would be to attempt in our own strength what God wants to do through us.

Guiding Spirit

A man was traveling through a thick forest. Although he had a compass, he did not check it, for he thought he knew the woods very well. Eventually, he took it out and was surprised to find he was going east instead of west.

Positive his instincts were right, he was about to throw the compass away. But it had never failed him, so he decided to trust it and changed direction. He reached his destination.

---

*Tape-recorded sermon delivered to ministers in the 1958 Sacramento, California crusade, reported in the *Pentecostal Evangel*, May 10, 1959.

Our instincts and inclinations can be poor guides. We must trust the Holy Spirit for guidance.

If Ananias had obeyed his inclinations, he would never have gone to "the street which is called Straight" (Acts 9:11). In his vision he protested that Saul of Tarsus had persecuted the saints and had come to imprison such as he. Nevertheless, he obeyed the voice of the Spirit.

Ananias went to the house of Judas and said, "Brother Saul, the Lord, even Jesus, that appeared unto thee . . . hath sent me" (v. 17). Only God knows the effect this Spirit-led, compassionate witness had on the life and ministry of Paul then and throughout his earthly pilgrimage. At the judgment seat of Christ Ananias will surely be there with "Brother Saul" to receive eternal reward.

Who was Ananias? One of the apostles? a prophet? an elder in the congregation of saints in Damascus? The Bible simply identifies him as "a certain disciple at Damascus." Just one of the members. But one who submitted to the leadership of the Holy Spirit.

God is not looking for great men. In fact, one dedicated minister remarked, "I didn't amount to very much until I learned that God did not expect me to be great." God is looking for humble men submissive to the voice of the Holy Spirit and seeking Him and trusting Him for guidance.

The Anointing Spirit

Andrew Bonar once said there will not be a redeemed person in heaven who does not have a human thumbprint on him. For example, Peter, who won thousands, was led to Christ by his brother Andrew.

The Holy Spirit's leadership is usually redemptive. That is, the leadership of the Spirit is most generally, either directly or indirectly, related to the salvation of souls. Even when He gives direction in a personal matter, it is to conform us to the image of Christ, the Master Soul Winner. The Holy Spirit will lead those who want to bring others to Christ today as surely as He led men in past ages.

One night a young woman was unable to sleep. This was unusual, so like the child Samuel she whispered, "Speak, Lord. . . ." He did. There was a poor family nearby whom everyone avoided. Then she fell asleep.

After many excuses the next morning, she walked down the street with a heavy heart. But after introducing herself to the mother in that home, the load lifted. She read the Bible and testified about the love of God for erring men.

The two women walked out on the porch where the husband had fled. The wife began to repeat all the things the visitor had told her.

After a while the godly woman asked the man if he was a Christian. When he replied negatively, she began to quote Scripture verses, some of which she had never memorized. Under the anointing of the Holy Spirit, she explained the plan of salvation.

Before long, there on the porch, the man fell to his knees saying, "I'm ready to give my heart to God." The three prayed together, and another Christian home graced the community.

Many years before, Peter avoided certain people. But God said to him in a vision: "What God hath cleansed, that call not thou common" (Acts 10:15). In obedience Peter went to the home of Cornelius to preach Christ. And the door of faith was opened to the Gentiles.

The Omnipotent Spirit

The soul winner is engaged in supernatural work. It is imperative that he be supernaturally led.

Who could know Saul the persecutor was a chosen vessel open to a Spirit-anointed ministration? Who could know a spiritually hungry Ethiopian would pass a certain spot at a certain time? Or who could know a friendless outcast would be hitchhiking in Indiana?

After waiting several hours for a ride, a young Christian hitchhiker started walking. He overtook a younger boy, and they became buddies immediately. The boy said he was 16 years old, and he hoped to find employment in the wheat fields of Nebraska.

Sitting down to rest under a large tree, the believer offered to share his lunch. He asked his newfound friend to pray and thank God for His provisions. The boy didn't know how to pray.

While they ate, the godly youth began to talk about the love of God and the plan of salvation. He had a receptive audience. They bowed their heads, and, faintly at first, then growing louder and more confident, the boy prayed for mercy and pardon.

Later the outcast smiled for the first time. His face seemed to shine. He explained: that morning his stepfather had told him to leave home. He had walked all day with nothing to eat. Surely no one cared, and he decided to jump off a bridge into the first river he came to. "But now," he exclaimed, "I feel so light! The heavy burden and weight inside me are gone."

God leads in different ways. The angel of the Lord told Philip to leave Samaria and head for the road from Jerusalem to Gaza. Why? The angel didn't say.

Ananias had a vision.

Today we would say providential circumstances brought two youths together in Indiana.

But really, these spiritual needs were met because God found people who were sensitive to His voice. The Holy Spirit knows the who, where, and when of needy thousands today. He needs believers sensitive to the still, small voice in the heart, to an impression deep in the soul, to a Spirit-created circumstance.

The Convicting Spirit

When Jesus promised to send the Holy Spirit, He added: "And when he is come, he will reprove [convict] the world of sin, and of righteousness, and of judgment" (John 16:8). Conviction is that work of the Holy Spirit that makes the unbeliever aware of his sinful condition in the sight of the Lord. He realizes that a God of undying love has no recourse but to pronounce judgment upon him. Such conviction is likely to result in genuine conversion.

A 17-year-old boy, under conviction, opened his heart: "When I think of becoming a man and facing the dreadfulness of the world, the fear seems to be so overwhelming that I can hardly sleep at night. The thought of death makes me quiver, even though I know that life has to end.

"I have tried to give up the emotions of sin, but at the end of the day as I count the sins I have committed, I seem to know that even if those sins are less than the day before, they are just as bad.

"I believe I am ready to suffer the hardships of the Christian life in order to be set free from the uncertainties and fears of the world. I need help."

This boy needed the Scriptures which prove a loving God calls sinners to repentance and then freely forgives them. He needed a Spirit-led witness.

That young man expressed the innermost thoughts of thousands. They have heard the gospel. They have brushed aside sermon, testimony, and printed page with a "Not now. Some other time."

They know the road they travel leads to eternal death. They are fearful, sleepless at times, miserable. They are all of this because the goodness of God calls them to repentance through the convicting power of a faithful Holy Spirit.

God help us to walk in the Spirit. To speak a word in season to men who are weary of sin (Isaiah 50:4).

Revelation of the Spirit

Without the revelation of the Holy Spirit, no man can be saved. Every sinner stands in the shoes of Nicodemus. He cannot comprehend the new birth because it is a spiritual revelation and transformation. But when he comes contritely to the Cross in simple faith, the Holy Spirit reveals Jesus as Saviour and Lord. He is "born of the Spirit" (John 3:8).

Jesus promised the revelation of the Spirit: "No man knoweth who the Son is, but the Father; and who the Father is, but the Son, and he to whom the Son will reveal him" (Luke 10:22). And "when he, the Spirit of truth, is come, . . . he shall receive of mine, and shall show it unto you" (John 16:13, 14).

Since only the Holy Spirit can truly reveal Jesus to the human heart, it is imperative that every soul winner have "the spirit of wisdom and revelation in the knowledge of him" (Ephesians 1:17).

Six women gathered in a little church one Wednesday morning for prayer. That is, five prayed. The other—arthritic and badly crippled, discouraged, lukewarm—had been tempted to take her life. A spirit of joy and worship welled up within the five. Prompted by the Spirit, they arose simultaneously to lay hands on their needy friend. Someone rebuked Satan.

The sick woman cried for pardon and deliverance. And through the mighty power and revelation of the Holy Spirit she was saved and healed.

Without the Spirit's power man at his best is weak. With the Spirit's power the weakest can be strong.

7

Show Me!

Edmund Burke wrote, "Example is the school of mankind, and they will learn at no other."

It is ingrained in man's nature to be more affected by seeing than by hearing. It has been said that one retains 20 percent of what he hears and 60 percent of what he sees.

Neighbors, fellow employees, and friends listen when you speak about salvation through the Lord Jesus Christ. They may respect what they consider to be your opinions. So by the same token they feel entitled to their own views. A few are quite critical. But most have no chip on their shoulders. Mentally, they simply say, "Show me."

If you asked what they want to see in you, they would probably be at a loss for words. They just want to wait. If you really believe, if you are absolutely sold on your beliefs, somehow you will be different. You will not lead an ordinary life. Most of them won't try you, but they will surely watch when you are tried.

After all, you have been talking over the backyard fence and rubbing shoulders with them day after day. The routine of life has not changed. You have been there in many yesterdays. Chances are you will still be around in the tomorrows. "So what's the hurry?" they feel.

You say these are the closing days of time. Jesus is coming soon. But really, is there anything in your life-style (something they can see) that shows you are preparing for Christ's return? If you have increased your giving to the church, if you are praying more than ever for the lost—it is not visible to them.

The people you will influence for Christ by your example and behavior are those you have made your friends. They may think you are overly zealous, but they can find "no evil thing to say of you" (Titus 2:8). In many cases they want to believe you. They want you to live what you preach. They are not challenging you. Rather, some may be rooting for you. If you prove true, it tends to indicate the "religious life" may be for them. What you do, they can do.

Since you insist that they believe as you do, then they feel you owe it to them to show in life and deed that God's way is the best and only way. If your life is above reproach, it can lead to their conversion.

The Better Man

Napoleon Bonaparte said: "When I took command of the French Army in Italy, my extreme youth made it necessary for me to evince the utmost severity of morals. This was indispensable to enable me to sustain authority over men so greatly superior in age and experience. My supremacy could be retained only by proving myself a better man than any other in the army. Had I yielded to human weakness, I should have lost my power."*

Who was in command of the situation when Stephen was stoned? Who was the better man?

It could have seemed to be Saul of Tarsus. For the

---

*Elon Foster, *Windows for Sermons* (Grand Rapids: Baker Book House), illustration # 7387.

witnesses who stoned Stephen "laid down their clothes at" Saul's feet. Saul was a proud "Hebrew of the Hebrews . . . a Pharisee . . . touching the righteousness which is in the law, blameless" (Philippians 3:5, 6). But his morality paled into insignificance before the conduct of Stephen in his last earthly hour.

Over 25 years later Paul remembered, and he said: "When the blood of thy martyr Stephen was shed, I also was standing by, and consenting unto his death" (Acts 22:20). Surely Stephen's conduct contributed to the conversion of Saul.

A Christian refused to take offense at the belligerence of a fellow employee. It seemed the terrible-tempered one was forever involved in an argument, and he sometimes resorted to fisticuffs to prove he was the better man.

One day the believer returned good for evil by inviting the sinner to a Sunday School Rally Day. He was surprised that his invitation was accepted.

This was an opportunity the fighter rather welcomed. He had been curious for a long time. He wanted to know what made the believer so congenial and kind. And he was ready when the Christian came to pick him up.

They arrived 15 minutes before the service began, and the believer introduced his guest to his teacher and other members of the class. Although most knew the visitor only too well, they greeted him warmly. It was an unusual atmosphere for the sinner. In about a month Christian behavior and the Word got to him. He was converted. He became a better man because his friend was a living "epistle . . . known and read of all men" (2 Corinthians 3:2).

"No Comment"

The apostle Paul wrote: "Stop being stumbling

blocks to Jews or Greeks or to the church of God, just as I myself am in the habit of pleasing everybody in everything, not aiming at my own welfare but at that of as many people as possible, in order that they may be saved" (1 Corinthians 10:32, 33, Williams).

To be an unwitting stumbling block is to be a stumbling block none the less. It is possible to give offense in a hasty, unthinking word or opinion. Better to give a quiet and polite, "No comment, please," than to say the wrong thing.

For example, several men approached a Christian one morning and told the same story—a fellow employee and lay preacher allegedly had deserted his family. By the time he heard the fifth report his "I don't believe it" was less firmly put.

The man knew the Word: "In the mouth of two or three witnesses shall every word be established" (2 Corinthians 13:1). He had had the presence of mind to ask how the men had received their information. And it seemed to be coming from several different sources. But he also knew a man is innocent until proven guilty. And even if the story proved to be true, surely no one would blame him for trusting a Christian friend.

Finally, a sinner to whom he had been witnessing came to his desk. "Did you hear the story about the preacher? I know you did. What do you think?" his words tumbled out.

The Christian looked up into a tense, perhaps wistful face. "I don't believe it," he said.

The sinner heaved a big sigh and grinned. "I hoped—I just knew you'd say that," he said. "One of these days you'll see me in church."

He did. In fact, several years later his questioner was a Sunday school teacher. The story proved to be untrue. The incident was known throughout the shop, and others were more open to the gospel.

How careful we must be—to think twice before speaking, and to believe and accept no gossip about anyone. The concern we have for the absent one reflects the concern we have for the one who faces us. And he knows it!

Many sinners have a mental image of what constitutes true Christian behavior. They have not read Romans 12:2, but it expresses their demands of believers: "Be not conformed to this world: but be ye transformed by the renewing of your mind, that ye may prove what is that good, and acceptable, and perfect will of God."

Sinners expect the believer's behavior and life to be consistent. If there is a change, if they think he is beginning to live like the worldling, they are quick to cry "hypocrite." And they say to themselves, "I'm as good as he is."

A soul winner cannot take the attitude: "What I do is my business." Whether he realizes it or not, his life is an open book. People know when the doors of his church are open, and they expect him to be there. In fact, our attendance constitutes confession of our faith in Christ who said: "Whosoever therefore shall confess me before men, him will I confess also before my Father which is in heaven" (Matthew 10:32).

A complete stranger to a pastor was saved in the very first church service he attended. The minister was curious. The man seemed to come for salvation without any urging, as though it had been his purpose in coming to church.

When questioned, the man said: "Well, one of the families from this church lives about a mile down the road from me. I've watched them for years. They never miss church. Sun or rain, sleet or snow, they drive by my house, waving as they go. I decided if it is as important as that, I should attend church too.''

Convinced by the behavior and attitude of this Christian family, the new convert was just beginning to learn that consistent church attendance is one of the outward evidences of a transformed life. It is a natural for believers who have proved to themselves what the good and perfect will of God is.

This inner transformation puts peace and joy in human hearts (Ephesians 5:19, 20). It shows in simple ways—a smile, a wave of the hand, a cheery greeting.

Deeds of Love

Deeds are often door openers for soul winners.

The service in the county home had concluded. The church youth leader was about to leave when a man urged him to come pray for a dying man. The concerned one infrequently attended the meetings which were conducted every 2 weeks.

The Christian motioned for another believer to accompany him. They walked down the corridor and entered a pitifully small room where an emaciated black man lay on a cot—unconscious and alone. His eyes were rolled back in his head, and the death rattle was in his throat. His tongue was so swollen that it protruded from his mouth.

The godly youths linked arms, and one placed his hand on the cool, clammy brow. He bowed his lips close to the dying man's ear. Slowly and distinctly he prayed, humbly acknowledging that all of us have sinned. He thanked the Lord Jesus for His love for erring men, and he prayed for forgiveness. He pled for Christ to reveal himself to the sick brother in love and mercy and grace.

The youths felt constrained to wait a moment. They sensed the holy presence of God. The dying man moved. His eyes focused, and he looked up at them. With a wisp of a smile he raised a feeble hand—grasped and pressed their fingers. Then he lapsed into a coma. He died that night.

Standing in the doorway was the concerned sinner who had urged them to come. He walked away without a word, with bowed head. In a later service he raised his hand when the appeal was given to accept Christ.

God knows the end from the beginning. Nothing takes Him by surprise. He prepares opportunities for us to show our faith by our works, by deeds of kindness. (See James 2:17-20.) But we must be willing to lay aside other plans. We must be available. We must walk in the Spirit so that we do and say the right thing at the right time.

"As he [Christ] is, so are we in this world" (1 John 4:17). He is a God of love and tender compassion. And He is pleased to reveal those attributes through adopted sons of God.

The Bigger Incentive

Your success as a soul winner depends on your motive.

In an old fable a dog bragged about his ability as a runner. One day he chased a rabbit and failed to catch it. The other dogs ridiculed him because of his previous boasting. He replied, "You must remember that the rabbit was running for his life while I was only running for my dinner." Somehow the dog could get another meal. The rabbit had only one life to live. The incentive was all-important.

If you are moved to do good deeds because it is the right thing to do or because it makes you feel good to be helpful, you are doing them "for your dinner"—for an earthly reason. Oh, people are grateful. They may even say, "He's a nice fellow." But the power to stir men to a change in heart and life is lacking. You need a deeper and eternal motive.

On the Damascus road Paul was moved to serve Jesus Christ. He determined to be "all things to all men, that [he] might by all means save some" (1 Corinthians 9:22). His deeds were done so that men might see Jesus in and through him.

A man was trying to lead a better life in his own strength. For one thing, he quit smoking. Several months later he didn't feel well at times. His doctor examined him and even sent him to the hospital for tests. They gave him a clean bill of health. But he still had physical complaints. He told a Christian fellow employee all this. It was evident he was worried.

The Christian was sympathetic. The odd thing was—he had had much the same symptoms. So he told what natural means he had used to relieve tension. Since he was not a doctor, he made no further suggestions.

So far, his concern and helpfulness were earthly. An opportunity to witness, an opportunity with a deeper motivation, remained—to tell the whole story: his union with the Saviour, his daily commital unto Him, and the abiding consciousness of His love and tender care, causing worries and tension to yield to the peace of God which passes understanding.

Listen . . .

Listening is an art, an important skill that many people never master.

An 11-year-old turned in a composition titled "Ears." In part, he wrote: "Ears were made to hear with, but some people use them for many other things. My grandmother's ears help keep her glasses on. My little brother's ears keep his hat from falling down over his eyes, and my sister's ear is usually glued to the telephone. I don't think she really listens though because she never stops talking long enough to hear what the other person is saying."

Some adults seem to love to hear the sound of their own voices. But every book on success devotes considerable space to listening to others. The successful soul winner must have a patient spirit; a willingness to listen to the outpourings of lonely hearts.

A so-called juvenile delinquent sent a letter to his parents. They, in turn, sent it to the local newspaper hoping to "help other parents."

Quoting from the young man's letter: "You asked me why I did those things and why I gave you so much trouble, and the answer is easy for me to give you, but I am wondering if you will understand.

"Remember when I was six or seven and I used to want you to listen to me? I remember all the nice things you gave me for Christmas and my birthday . . . but the rest of the time during the year . . . I just wanted you to listen to me like I was somebody who felt things too. But you said you were too busy.

"If anybody asks where I am, tell them I've gone looking for somebody with time because I've got a lot of things I want to talk about."

This letter not only represents the feelings of many in the coming generation but also the now generation. You meet them every day—people who have seldom found another willing to listen.

Witnessing is more than telling. You can talk and fail to get the sinner's attention. Witnessing is a two-way street. It is communication. For sure, you have the sinner's attention if he talks to you.

In 1 Timothy 4:12, we read: "Be thou an example of the believers . . . in spirit"—a spirit that signals to lonely hearts that you have time to listen.

8

True Experiences Linger

The Simple Truth

"Jesus Christ has changed my life."

This was the oft-repeated testimony of a university freshman. Although his I.Q. had opened the doors of higher learning to him, his ignorance of the Bible was appalling.

Reared in a godless home, he had never attended Sunday school. God's name was an expletive to use when adjectives failed to convey surprise, dismay, or anger. But one day a "chance" turn of the dial tuned him in on a radio sermon. Something the pastor said attracted his attention momentarily, and then he listened—captivated by the message. Later, he visited the speaker and yielded to the Lord.

Jesus became real to him. "He's changed my life," he said.

Not all Christians can preach or teach. But all believers can testify—tell their personal experience with God. Personal testimony is a powerful weapon for soul winning. It has a way of wakening the disinterested, inspiring the inquirer, and disarming the argumentative. It can linger in the soul like good seed in the soil—and eventually bring forth fruit.

Effective testimony does two things: it tells what was done and who did it. It transports the hearer's attention from the secular to the spiritual and from earth to heaven. It turns the eye of the inquirer from the transformed sinner to the divine Changer of hearts and lives.

That's exactly what the newborn but spiritually illiterate youth's testimony did. What was done? His life was changed. Who did it? Jesus Christ.

The apostle Paul put it this way: "Christ Jesus entered the world to rescue sinners. I realize that I was the worst of them all" (1 Timothy 1:15, Phillips).

Truth vs. Error

The believer's testimony of his personal contact with Jesus Christ attracts the attention of most sinners. It was so with the Samaritans when the woman returned from Jacob's Well excitedly crying, "Come here, look at a man who has told me everything I ever did! Can he be the Christ?" No further urging was needed—"They set out from the town on their way to him" (John 4:29, 30, Moffatt).

Neither could the university freshman's vibrant testimony be lightly shrugged off. His roommate was a communist. They frequently engaged in bedtime discussions on the respective merits of communism and Christianity.

The young Christian wisely visited his pastor occasionally because he "needed to learn a lot." He ruefully said he did not know the answers, and his roommate could "talk him into a corner any time." But with confidence in his eyes he said, "I keep telling him Jesus has changed my life."

Towards the end of the semester the unbelieving youth had to face up to the fact that his fellow student was not putting on an act. His belief in the unseen Christ was genuine. His vibrant joy indicated some sort of an almost personal relationship. He became so curious he went to the pastor of his roommate and said,

"I want to know just how Jesus Christ can change a person's life."

The communist was merely curious, not convicted of his sins. But several weeks later he returned for another talk in the pastor's study. This time he was converted. The personal testimony of a personal relationship with Jesus bore fruit.

No soul winner knows all the answers. But he knows his darkness has turned to light. And he can say: "One thing I know, that, whereas I was blind, now I see" (John 9:25).

Truth and Honesty

On the other hand, the witness does not belong on a pedestal. Rather than "talking down" to sinners, he must identify himself with them. Christ did.

The Lord "made himself of no reputation, and took upon him the form of a servant, and was made in the likeness of men: and being found in fashion as a man, he humbled himself, and became obedient unto death, even the death of the cross" (Philippians 2:7, 8). Christ identified himself with His creatures so that He might bring "many sons unto glory" (Hebrews 2:10).

An elderly street vendor was an avowed atheist. When a Christian gave his personal testimony, the old man boasted: "In all my sixty years, I have never read the Bible, entered the doors of a church, or listened to a sermon. I hate God. I think that religion is all superstition. There is no heaven nor hell."

Surprised and distressed by this venomous outburst, the believer retreated. He prayed and asked other members of his church to pray.

The next day the Christian bought some vegetables from the old vendor. He checked his change and saw that a mistake had been made. "You shortchanged yourself five cents," he said. After returning that sum, he walked away.

The old atheist was startled. His vision was failing, and he wondered how many times he had been shortchanged before—and no one had been honest enough to tell him.

Now the personal testimony began to clamor for attention in the heart of the old sinner. The witness had identified himself with the unbeliever in showing concern for him. The elderly man was in church that evening, but he slipped out just before the conclusion of the meeting. However, a strange compulsion brought him back to the revival services night after night. Awful conviction for sin came upon his soul. He yielded to Christ about 2 weeks after hearing the personal testimony that provoked him.

Divine Connection

God provides opportunities to witness. But soul winners can miss them unless they are alert and sensitive to the leading of the Holy Spirit.

A Los Angeles Christian tried to telephone his sister in Pennsylvania. Something went wrong. Instead, he heard two strangers talking. A lonely man was pleading for reconciliation with his wife and children.

About to hang up and dial again, the believer felt a check in his spirit. Perhaps God had brought him into this unhappy situation.

The wife and mother said it had taken a long time for her to decide to make the break, and having made it, she was through. Although the children were having difficulty making the adjustment, she felt the separation was best for all of them.

The husband knew his alcoholism had been responsible. He admitted to many promises to stop drinking, but now he realized his family meant more to him than the bottle. This time he was determined to quit. In fact, he already had.

At this point the believer interrupted. He identified himself and explained that he had tried to dial his sister in Altoona. Somehow he had been connected with this conversation between a steel executive in Pittsburgh and his wife in Huntington. The man was angry. His wife sobbed quietly.

Speaking as a Christian, the Los Angeles man felt this meeting had been arranged by the Lord. He said he sensed deep contrition and determination in the husband's voice. He knew God would help them, if they would give Him a chance. And he urged them to be reconciled.

Several weeks later, he received a letter from Pittsburgh. The family had been reunited, and they were confident God would help them work everything out.

Godly Strangers

Opportunities to witness present themselves on the job, in the routine of daily living. It may be neither desirable nor wise to make lengthy, daily appeals to accept Christ. The continual concern evidenced by a few words as occasion permits will impress the sinful heart.

The little maid in Naaman's home was a captive in a strange land. Perhaps she had no hope of ever seeing parents or friends again. She could have been dejected, thinking the God of Israel had forgotten and forsaken her and her family. But God-given faith and concern for others remained in her heart.

Of course, the young slave girl knew her master was a leper. One day she mustered the courage to approach her mistress and speak out. "Would God my lord were with the prophet that is in Samaria!" she said. "For he would recover him of his leprosy'' (2 Kings 5:3). Naaman went. He was healed. And he became a worshiper of the true and living God (vv. 17, 18).

A young unmarried Christian knew his employer wished to send someone from his department to a branch factory in another city. Although it was only a 3-month tour-of-duty, no one wanted to go. He didn't like the idea either, but somehow he found himself accepting the assignment.

He secured lodging in a private home. During the first week he learned parents and children never attended Sunday school or church. He asked his landlady where the nearest Assembly of God was located, and he attended the services

This opened the door to further conversation, and he gave his personal testimony. Before he returned to his regular job, the wife and mother was converted and the entire family was attending Sunday school. Oh, he knew why he had been impressed to comply with his employer's wishes.

Time to Think

When people are troubled or ill, when they have time to think, they sense their need of something surpassing natural means and human resources. They may well be open and receptive to a personal testimony, to a personal encounter with Jesus Christ.

The sick can take heart from the healing of the woman with an issue of blood. If she had not reached the end of human resources, would she have pressed through the crowd to touch the hem of the Master's garment? (Luke 8:43-48).

A woman heard her pastor invite people to come to the altar for prayer, people who wanted healing not only for personal relief but also to win others to Christ through their personal testimony. She went forward, and the Lord delivered her.

The following morning the budding witness remembered an unsaved acquaintance she had not seen in about a year. She called this friend, and a baby sitter said she was in the hospital.

Conscious that God was leading her, the Christian went to the hospital. She testified about her healing and said Christ would heal the sick woman too—if she would trust Him. It didn't happen.

However, the godly woman kept in touch after her friend was released from the hospital. Finally, she prevailed on the sinner and her husband to attend church. They were converted that night.

Jesus was so real and wonderful to this newborn couple. They just had to tell all their friends about His saving grace. Within a month this husband-and-wife team led 23 people to Christ!

Christ sent forth His disciples to minister by twos. Solomon said: "Two are better than one, because they have a good (more satisfying) reward for their labor; for if they fall, the one will lift up his fellow" (Ecclesiastes 4:9, 10, *The Amplified Bible*).

Making Opportunities

Simon the Pharisee invited Jesus to a feast in his home. In so doing he unwittingly provided an opportunity for the Lord to reveal himself as the Forgiver of sins. To Simon and his guests, Jesus said: "I say unto thee, Her sins, which are many, are forgiven; for she loved much: but to whom little is forgiven, the same loveth little." And to the sinful woman the Lord said, "Thy sins are forgiven" (Luke 7:47, 48).

Modern people intentionally create opportunities to witness to the Saviour in their homes. A family in the West has made a habit of inviting unsaved guests to their home for the Friday evening meal. They also invite one Christian couple or more. In a very casual and relaxed atmosphere and without forcing, the conversation frequently turns to the unseen Guest in every Christian home.

Opportunities to testify are given in street meetings. One man was under conviction due to the personal testimony of a man on the job. He tried to hide it and act as if he were unmoved.

The sinner knew his Christian friend was at a street meeting every Saturday evening. There in the darkness hiding behind a big maple tree, he listened. Once in a while he brushed a tear from his eye. It took several years, but he finally yielded to Christ.

Christians can make opportunities in church. One member saw a man sitting at pew end with his chin cupped in his hand. He was watching his wife who had gone to the altar for salvation. The believer approached, leaned down, and quietly said, "God loves you too."

They were the right words. The sinner got out of that seat and rushed to the altar. Those few words turned a possibly divided home into a united home—one in Christ Jesus.

Christ came "to seek and to save that which was lost" (Luke 19:10). In His stead we should seek opportunities to witness to sinful men.

Grasp the Advantage

Sinners may shrug off the preacher's message as "just another sermon. That's his job. He's paid to do it." They may lightly receive the teacher's lesson as "just another man's idea. That's what *he* thinks!"

Here, the witness has the advantage. Testifying, by no stretch of the imagination, can be termed a sermon, a job, or an idea. The witness is not paid. The sinner under conviction uneasily thinks, "What makes him do this?" The testifier is not a purveyor of ideas. He testifies to fact, personal experience. In effect, he says, "I know that my Redeemer liveth" (Job 19:25).

Sinners may think, "Sunday school is for kids," and they refuse to listen to the teaching of the Word. Men who regard preaching as "just another profession" seldom hear a sermon. But these same people gladly listen to a sincere testimony.

Christian employees have proved this. In the snack area at break or lunchtime two or more believers can begin talking about what Christ has done for them personally, about the conversion of a friend, relative, or fellow employee, or about a recent miraculous healing.

Sinners may try to veil their interest, but they will listen in. A chair may be moved closer. A man may go for a cup of coffee and return to a chair nearer the center of conversation. And away from the crowd, a listener will approach one of the believers and confess his interest.

The personal testimony is accepted in a vast variety of settings: in the high government office and in the ghetto, in school and on the job, in the hospital and on the athletic field. The Fellowship of Christian Athletes numbers over 100,000. They emphasize the personal testimony.

The personal testimony is accepted in heaven as the offering of a grateful heart. It boomerangs to bless the witness himself. Again, he has recalled and recounted the wonder and joy of his own conversion. His faith and the convictions of his soul have been strengthened in the telling. He feels just a little closer to God and man.

9

Teaching Evangelism

Awakening

In 1954, by joint resolution of Congress, the Pledge of Allegiance to our flag was amended by the addition of the words "under God." President Eisenhower stated that the addition of this phrase reaffirmed "the transcendence of religious faith in America's heritage and future."

True, our country is blessed with a religious heritage. In the Mayflower Compact the Pilgrims wrote that they had come to establish a colony "for the glory of God, and advancement of the Christian faith. . . ."

During the Great Awakening of the 1740s, George Whitefield and others called the colonists to repentance. When he preached in Philadelphia, the saloons had to close. The founding fathers of our nation were influenced and inspired by this great spiritual move.

They concluded their Declaration of Independence with these words: "With a firm reliance on the protection of Divine Providence, we mutually pledge to each other our Lives, our Fortunes, and our sacred Honor."

John Adams, one of the signers and later president of our country, wrote: "It is religion and morality alone upon which freedom can securely stand. A patriot must be a religious man."

Later, our founding fathers drew up our Constitution. The First Amendment to the Bill of Rights guarantees us freedom of religion. They believed: "Blessed is the nation whose God is the Lord" (Psalm 33:12). And on our coins they put, "In God we trust."

America stands in need of another Great Awakening, a time of individual and national repentance, a time of revival. Revival is first an individual matter which can spread like fire. God help us to spark a great move of the Holy Spirit.

The future is in the hands of God. But, under God, we can share in molding the future. The "faith of our fathers" was instilled in many colonial children by Pilgrims and Puritans who built schools and made the Bible their first textbook.

That faith in a God of undying love who is not willing that any should perish, that faith in the righteous Judge of all the earth, must be instilled in this generation. "Faith cometh by hearing, and hearing by the word of God" (Romans 10:17). It must be taught. And every Christian is under divine orders to teach it.

More Certain Results

The closest, most important, and finest soul-winning-teaching opportunity available to the average Christian is in the home. God knows there is no more fertile soil than the heart of a child. And His Word commands: "Thou shalt love the Lord thy God with all thine heart. . . . And these words, which I command thee this day, shall be in thine heart: and thou shalt teach them diligently unto thy children . . ." (Deuteronomy 6:5-7).

Timothy's grandmother, Lois, and his mother, Eunice, taught him. The apostle Paul wrote: "From a child thou hast known the holy Scriptures, which are able to make thee wise unto salvation through faith which is in Christ Jesus" (2 Timothy 3:15). The soul-winning teacher, then, not only tells others about

Christ but also tries to introduce them to a personal, intimate, and loving Saviour.

A godly mother lived in her daughter's home for the last 25 years of her life. In that home, she alone knew the Lord. However, her son-in-law was very kind. He took her, his son, and his daughter to church every Sunday. The children grew up, married, and established their own homes. They were still unsaved. It seemed the old saint's ministry in that home was fruitless.

This saintly woman died at 94 years of age—at peace with God and man. She was a faithful attendant and active in church work until the last few weeks of her life. Like the worthies in Hebrews 11, she died in faith, and that faith was rewarded.

Several years later, her daughter was converted. A few more years passed, and the granddaughter was saved. This young woman has an immense living room, and she began to invite neighbors and friends into her home for afternoon prayer meetings. It was not unusual to have 50 people in attendance.

Souls were saved and baptized in the Holy Spirit. This news spread to the grandson's home, 2,000 miles away. The great-grandson began to attend church and was converted. Now the grandson is attending church regularly for the first time since he was married. And recently, the godly saint's kind son-in-law, a man in his seventies, was saved.

Although teaching may appear less glamorous than other methods of soul winning, and although its fruit may be less rapidly reaped, its results are more certain and more abundant.

The Exact Words

Jesus said to His disciples: "Go ye therefore, and teach . . ." (Matthew 28:19). They did—in the temple and in homes. "They, continuing daily with one accord in the temple, and breaking bread from house to house, did eat their meat with gladness and singleness of heart . . . and the Lord added to the church daily" (Acts 2:46, 47). And "in every house, they ceased not to teach and preach Jesus Christ" (5:42). The early believers taught Christ in their own homes and in every home that opened its doors to them.

Today, when doors are opened willingly to soul winners, it usually indicates the hosts appreciate the visit and their guests' concern. Being in their own home, they are less likely to be ill-at-ease and more likely to be open to the gospel.

However, one rather surly man invited a witnessing duo into his home. The TV was on, and the room was quite dark. The host told them to be seated on the sofa. Then he turned off the TV and flicked the light switch. Then he proceeded to tell them what was wrong with pastors and churches.

The Christians kept their cool. After all, they were presenting Christ, not their church or any other. The leader sensed it would be wise to be pleasant, to give the man his undivided attention, and to trust the Holy Spirit to guide him.

Finally, the soul winner got a chance to say that Jesus loved his host; that in the Book of Revelation Jesus said: "Behold, I stand at the door, and knock: if any man hear my voice, and open the door, I will come in to him, and will sup with him, and he with me" (3:20).

The sinner became quite agitated and rose to his feet, signifying the visit was over. At the door as the soul winners turned to say, "Good-bye," they looked toward the sofa. There on the wall was a picture of Christ knocking on the door. Until that moment they had not known it was there, and they realized the Holy

Spirit had given the exact words to pierce the heart of the sinner. Who can tell the thoughts of his heart? Who can tell what the results will be?

Public Satisfaction

People who are convicted of their sins, people who are saved at home or in another's home, must be steered into the church. There the teaching ministry can be more fully utilized. With no secular interruptions, with opportunity to ask questions, the seeker after truth can find deliverance, help, and guidance. United with others of like precious faith, he can grow in the knowledge of Jesus Christ.

This is good—as it should be—but the need of the lost still compels the church to reach out beyond its four walls. Asked why his growing Sunday school and church could progress as it evidently was without a fleet of buses, a member explained. On the first Sunday a child attended, the teacher secured his name and address. This was for the teacher's information—he visited the child. But he also turned that information over to a visitation committee. One week two members would visit the parents. The next week two others would visit in the child's home.

"We have been very successful in winning families," the Christian said. "A child has a transportation problem. But families usually furnish their own transportation."

Another church ran a small fleet of buses. They picked up children in a tiny mountain village. In time, some of them were converted, and they told neighbors and friends about their Saviour.

An almost destitute woman in her late forties lived alone in a small shack. One Sunday she boarded the bus with the children. If the people in church noticed she was poorly dressed, they didn't show it. She was welcomed by Christians and by their Saviour.

After this newborn believer was baptized in water several months later, she choked back the tears and told her pastor how thankful she was for the bus. "I would never have found the Lord if you folks had not brought me in," she said.

Just one such incident pays for a fleet of buses!

The apostle Paul said: "I kept back nothing that was profitable unto you, but have showed you, and have taught you publicly . . . repentance toward God, and faith toward our Lord Jesus Christ" (Acts 20:20, 21). People will never be satisfied in God until they have made public confession of their faith.

Know the Author

What are the requirements for soul-winning teaching?

The apostle Paul said: "I thank Christ Jesus our Lord, who hath enabled me, for that he counted me faithful, putting me into the ministry" (1 Timothy 1:12). He further advised Timothy: "What you heard me say before many witnesses entrust to faithful people who will be able to teach others" (2 Timothy 2:2, *Beck*).

The soul-winner teacher must be faithful. If his car started four out of five times, if his watch ran 23 out of 24 hours, would he consider them faithful? Certainly not.

We must "be instant [ready] in season, out of season" (2 Timothy 4:2). We must "be ready always to give an answer to every man that asketh you a reason of the hope that is in you, with meekness and fear" (1 Peter 3:15).

Faithful to whom? An individual? a Sunday school class? the Scriptures? Yes. But one who is faithful spiritually has first learned to be faithful to the Creator of individuals, to the Author of the Bible. He is faithful to Christ because he knows Him. And because he knows the Lord, he has consistent, personal fellowship with Him.

Through the years a young Christian had distributed a certain tract. Of course, the author's name and address appeared at the conclusion. He also had read this man's articles in various religious publications. One day he decided to visit him. Greeted at the door by a rather ordinary, oldish man, he was somewhat disappointed. But he received a gracious and friendly invitation to come in.

After a few minutes of conversation, the visitor wondered why he had considered his host just ordinary. As they talked about Jesus and the wonders of His grace, the older man's face became animated. His voice sometimes choked with love and emotion. Before leaving the young Christian urged the author to visit him.

The young man had used the tracts, had read the articles with profit, but after meeting the author, he loved him and desired more fellowship with him.

We bring into our teaching ministry the assurance, the joy, the love, and the essence of Christ's presence which years of fellowship have woven into the fabric of our being. Marion Lawrence said, "A teacher teaches more by what he is than by what he says or does."

Scared to Teach

Christ gave the invitation: "Come unto me . . . and learn of me" (Matthew 11:28, 29). But He also inspired the apostle to write: "Study to show thyself approved unto God, a workman that needeth not to be ashamed, rightly dividing the word of truth" (2 Timothy 2:15). We cannot teach others more then we ourselves have learned. So we must faithfully study and prepare ourselves for the teaching ministry.

A young Christian had received some "on-the-job-training" in a Sunday school class with an experienced teacher. He anticipated becoming an assistant teacher.

Then a guest minister preached about the responsibilities of parents, teachers, and adult Christians to our youth. He challenged teachers, particularly, to prepare their lessons more thoroughly, aiming to involve pupils by questions, comments, and putting the lesson into practice.

Later the prospective teacher approached his older instructor saying, "That sermon scared me. Teaching is, as he said, a great responsibility. Can I prepare lessons as thoroughly as the minister said we should? Will I have the answer to pupils' questions?" Oh, he was upset and ready to quit.

The teacher explained that scaring his hearers was farthest from the minister's mind and intentions. The Christian life itself is a high and holy calling. But after praying in the morning, believers are not afraid to face people and the problems of the day.

Here, the teacher had an advantage. He knew his assistant well, and he concluded: "You let people at your place of employment know which side of the fence you're on. So pray, prepare, and do your best. God will supply the enabling and the guidance you need."

The young assistant proved those words. In several months he had his own class of primaries.

No teacher can ever be sure he knows exactly how the lesson must be presented. Only God knows the trial a pupil, young or old, faces. Only God knows the new or long-absent student who will be there—and the perplexing question he might ask. The teacher can follow his outline or plan and still depend on the Holy

Spirit to inspire him to present the truth that will supply a need or lead a soul to Christ.

Sure Reward

Shall not he who perseveres, shall not he who radiates the presence of Christ be rewarded? The Psalmist wrote: "He that goeth forth and weepeth, bearing precious seed, shall doubtless come again with rejoicing, bringing his sheaves with him" (Psalm 126:6).

Late one Saturday evening a pastor was working and praying in preparation for the morrow. He answered his phone and could hear only the sound of a woman sobbing. Then he recognized the voice of one of his finest Sunday school teachers: "Pastor, forgive me for calling you at this late hour. But my heart is so burdened for the boys in my class that I feel I can't live unless God saves them. Please, Pastor—please pray for them."

Moses interceded for his erring people: "Oh, this people have sinned a great sin. . . . Yet now, if thou wilt forgive their sin—; and if not, blot me, I pray thee, out of the book which thou hast written" (Exodus 32:31, 32). Christ himself wept over Jerusalem crying: "How often would I have gathered thy children together . . ." (Matthew 23:37). And He promised: "If two of you shall agree on earth as touching any thing that they shall ask, it shall be done for them of my Father which is in heaven" (18:19).

That night the pastor and teacher agreed in prayer. The next morning, in Christ's stead and imbued with His compassion, that godly woman taught Christ crucified. Eight boys, every member of her class, came to Jesus.

A joyful reward for a soul-winning teacher.

10
Lay Preachers

In the Will of God

Henry Drummond wrote:* "The end of life is not to do good, although many think so. It is not to win souls, although I once thought so. The end of life is—to do the will of God.

"A young minister in a small church, on a small salary, who has a wife and five children, received a tempting offer to go on the lecture platform. He replied, 'The Lord never called me to lecture, but to preach the gospel'—and dismissed the matter from his mind.

"The maximum achievement of any man's life, after it is all over, is to have done the will of God. No Luther, no Spurgeon, no Wesley can have done any more with their lives; and a dairy maid or a road laborer can do as much."

Jesus commanded the apostles "that they should not depart from Jerusalem, but wait for the promise of the Father" (Acts 1:4). They obeyed and were baptized in the Holy Spirit. Then Peter preached to the multitude, and 3,000 were saved. He had begun to obey Jesus' command: "Go ye into all the world, and preach the gospel to every creature" (Mark 16:15). Peter realized the will of God was all-important.

---

*Pentecostal Evangel, 1953.

"Believers were the more added to the Lord, multitudes both of men and women. . . . And daily in the temple, and in every house, they ceased not to teach and preach Jesus Christ" (Acts 5:14, 42). After the death of Stephen, "There was a great persecution against the church which was at Jerusalem; and . . . they that were scattered abroad went every where preaching the word" (8:1, 4).

Lay members of the Early Church preached in the temple and in homes, to crowds and to individuals. So what is preaching? Does it always involve a preacher, pulpit, audience, and sermon? Not always. What constitutes an audience? Christ preached to one woman at Jacob's Well. And He had no pulpit, no organ, no choir, no church.

"Preach" is from the Greek *euaggelizo*, meaning: to announce good news (evangelize), to bring glad tidings, declare, proclaim. Early Christians announced the good news of the gospel. They proclaimed Jesus of Nazareth as Lord and Saviour. They walked in His will.

Preachers Without a Pulpit

Philip was a deacon, not an apostle, but he preached to individuals in Jerusalem. Then he went to Samaria. "The people with one accord gave heed unto those things which Philip spake" (Acts 8:6). And there was a great revival. In the midst of this bountiful harvest the angel of the Lord told the evangelist to go to the road between Jerusalem and Gaza. He obeyed and preached Christ to the Ethiopian eunuch. A lay member of the church, a chariot for a pulpit, an audience of one—Philip did the will of God.

One dedicated layman has a knack few Christians acquire. He can meet a total stranger and within 5 minutes preach Christ to him. He does not need a point of contact. He is so pleasant and Christlike that it must seem almost natural to sinners to hear him ask, "Are you a Christian? Have you been born again?"

This exceptional soul winner was contented—working in his church and letting his light shine on the job. Well-meaning, sincere church members and fellow employees told him many times that he should be a minister. Finally, they and his family convinced him.

Having attended only part of the first year of high school, he had a rough time in Bible college. Three years passed, and he could not be graduated with his class because he had flunked English. This man who could converse so well with sinners! He attended another year and was graduated.

This fine Christian accepted a pastorate. But he soon felt ill-at-ease and out-of-place. He remembered that many times through the years when friends had urged him to prepare for the ministry, he got "butterflies in the stomach." He became nervous just thinking about it. Confiding to a friend, he said, "I should have known I wasn't 'cut out to be a pastor.' How was a dumb country boy to know the difference between an invitational and a worship hymn?"

So this dedicated soul winner is back on the job, preaching Christ to every sinner he meets. More effective than ever due to his training in the Word.

Many who preach do not have a pulpit. But they do the will of God, preaching Christ whenever and wherever they find a soul willing to listen.

Declaring the Unknown God

When we give our personal testimony to an individual, and he walks away without comment or question (which is unusual), we have had no opportunity to teach or preach. But if he asks a question about our conversion, then in our reply we instruct or teach him.

If the sinner thinks his best merits God's approval and heaven, then we must declare that "all our righteousnesses are as filthy rags" in the sight of God; that "there is none other name under heaven given among men, whereby we must be saved"; and, "Except ye repent, ye shall all likewise perish" (Isaiah 64:6; Acts 4:12; Luke 13:3). That is gospel truth. And whoever proclaims the good news of the gospel is a preacher.

What is the gospel?

It is perhaps best defined by the apostle Paul: "I declare unto you the gospel . . . how that Christ died for our sins according to the Scriptures; and that he was buried, and that he rose again the third day according to the Scriptures" (1 Corinthians 15:1-4).

Paul further wrote: "The preaching of the cross is to them that perish, foolishness. . . . It pleased God by the foolishness of preaching [of the things preached] to save them that believe" (1:18, 21).

Longinus, an ancient secular writer, called Paul "a master of unproved dogma." To worldly wise Greeks, God (if there was a God) would not reveal himself to man. They could not accept the supernatural, so the resurrection of Christ was a myth. And to preach that men could be saved by confessing their sins to a God who had died on a cross was utter foolishness.

Some modern people have much the same concept of God. Great sorrows and disappointments had broken the heart of a school teacher. She turned to agnosticism. But a Christian friend preached Christ crucified to her—a loving Saviour who desired to meet every need and longing of her heart. It was good news. News the teacher wanted to believe, and she accepted an invitation to attend church.

After listening to the preaching of Christ and Him

crucified for several weeks, the teacher said to the pastor, "I see it now."

Puzzled, the minister asked what it was she saw. And she gave this beautiful answer: "I see in Jesus we discover all of God we can know, and in Jesus we have all of God we can need." No longer did she believe that God is unknown and unknowable.

Keep It Simple

"Not many wise men after the flesh, not many mighty, not many noble, are called: but God hath chosen the . . . weak things of the world to confound the things which are mighty . . . that no flesh should glory in his presence. . . . As it is written, He that glorieth, let him glory in the Lord" (1 Corinthians 1:26-31).

God intended that the gospel of Christ be so simple anyone can preach it. D. L. Moody was uneducated.

A bright but critical physician went to hear Moody with no other idea than to have something to laugh at. He knew the preacher was not a scholar, and he felt sure he could find many flaws in his "argument."

Converted, he later explained: "I found I could not get at the man. He just stood there hiding behind the Bible and fired one Bible text after another at me till they went home to my heart straight as bullets from a rifle." So God and His Word were magnified, not D. L. Moody.

Many times the more simply the gospel is presented the more effective it is. Look at it in outline form:

A. Christ died for our sins.

B. He was buried.

C. He arose the third day.

D. He is able to save all who come unto God by Him.

This simple outline is the heart of Peter's messages on the Day of Pentecost, on the day the man was healed at the Beautiful Gate, and after his imprisonment. (See

Acts 2; 3; 4.) He was an unlearned and ignorant but Spirit-led fisherman.

A Christian met a man who had just come from a bar. He struck up a conversation and perceived that he was not under the influence of liquor. The believer said he had great news if the sinner had time to listen. "Sure," he replied. "Go ahead."

The soul winner said, "Jesus Christ died for your sins on the cross and arose again from the dead, and if you believe this with all your heart, He will save you from your sins."

The sinner studied the speaker for a long moment. Then he said quietly, "Sir, I believe that."

Asked if he would like to invite Jesus to come into his heart then and there, he replied, "I sure would." The sinner prayed for pardon and received the assurance of salvation.

A modern Christian preached Christ following the same simple outline and obtained the same results.

How You Say It

Most of the apostles were not educated enough to use "enticing words of man's wisdom" in their ministries. Although Paul could have done so, he wrote: "Our preaching of the good news came to you not entirely in words but with power and with the Holy Spirit and with absolute certainty (for you know the kind of men we were among you for your own sakes)" (1 Thessalonians 1:5, Williams).

Paul worked as a tentmaker to supply his needs and the needs of his fellow laborers. And the early Christians continued with their daily tasks. Sinners rubbed shoulders with them; they knew what manner of people the believers were, and they were influenced by their lives and dedication. The Christians actually practiced what they preached!

At Christmas, a Sunday school teacher gave a slide talk on the birth of Jesus. One of his most faithful pupils was sick, so he made arrangements to visit the lad and present the lesson again. When he arrived, he was thrilled to see the room crowded with neighborhood children, over half of whom did not attend Sunday school. The sick boy's father was absent and was not expected to return until late that night.

Halfway through his talk, the teacher sensed that someone had entered and was standing in the shadows beyond the doorway. He concluded the talk with three slides: the Crucifixion, the Resurrection, and Christ knocking on the door. With these last three slides he preached Christ to some children who had never attended Sunday school. He asked them all to bow their heads and join him in prayer at the conclusion.

As the teacher was packing his equipment preparatory to leaving, the father entered and shook hands. He confessed that he had entertained ill feelings for the visitor, and he apologized. He now knew that the teacher understood and loved children. He knew the teacher really meant what he said. The father came back to church and to God.

It has been said: "It is not so much what you say; it is how you say it." With love, sincerity, assurance, and in the power of the Holy Spirit.

Co-partners

J. Hudson Taylor, founder of the China Inland Mission, said: "I used to ask God if He would come and help me; and then I asked God if I might help Him; and then I ended by asking God to do His own work through me."

The Lord works through yielded vessels by the Holy Spirit. Paul said his preaching was with power and with the Holy Spirit and with absolute certainty (1

Thessalonians 1:5). This is the only way to preach effectively. No matter how simple the outline, no matter how much we prepare and study, our efforts are in vain without the power of the Spirit. God must do His own work through us.

It is good to memorize key Scripture verses on salvation. But even if we have these verses at tongue-tip, even if we preach so logically that a sinner mentally accepts what we say, our efforts are still vain. "No man can come to me [Christ], except the Father which hath sent me draw him" (John 6:44). Sinners must be convicted in their heart of their sins and convinced of their need of Christ. This is the office work of the Holy Spirit.

Evangelist Gipsy Smith said: "Let every fiber of your being, every thought of your mind, every moment of the day, be kissed by the power of the Cross into the transparent, beautiful thing that God Almighty meant your life to be! He will lift you into partnership with Himself. The greatest honor that heaven confers on a human soul is to make him a co-partner with God, the Infinite, to save the world."*

The consciousness of the indwelling Spirit infuses great conviction and assurance in the preacher's heart, and this certainty is communicated by the Holy Spirit to the hearer's heart. People were unimpressed with the repetitious teaching of the scribes, but when Jesus spoke His audience was gripped, for He spoke with authority.

Jesus said: "Greater works than these shall he do; because I go unto my Father" (John 14:12). And "as he [Jesus] is, so are we in this world" (1 John 4:17). Modern preachers, co-partners with God, can depend

---

*Taken from the *Pentecostal Evangel*.

on the Word and upon the Holy Spirit to speak through them with an authority that is not of this world.

Scarcely a fourth of the usual midweek audience attended church due to adverse weather conditions and sickness. The godly pastor told his people he had long since determined to give his best to every gathering in every service. Then he preached a sermon that made everyone glad he had braved the elements. They knew their pastor had spent many hours in prayer and preparation, and they loved him!

The size of an audience must never govern our willingness and readiness to preach. Jesus put the value on a human soul when He said: "What shall it profit a man, if he shall gain the whole world, and lose his own soul?" (Mark 8:36). Since every soul is so precious to the individual and to God, then where is the small ministry? There is no small ministry or audience.

Young or old, rich or poor, moral or immoral—they deserve our concern and our best, under God.

A little 5-year-old knelt at the altar with his grandfather one Sunday evening. A young soul winner asked the elderly gentleman if the boy wanted to give his heart to Jesus. He replied rather curtly that the child did not comprehend what he was doing.

Immediately, the soul winner knelt beside the little fellow. Oh, yes, he wanted Jesus to come into his heart. And later, he knew Jesus had forgiven him. To this day, some 30 years later, there is a bond of love between the soul winner and the boy he helped to Jesus.

This points up the fact that every opportunity to lead a soul to Christ should be grasped. No God-given audience should slip from us without hearing the message of salvation. And the transaction is never complete until the wandering sheep is in the fold.

11
The Master Shows How

When a question of policy arises in private industry, the lower echelons search for rulings from the "front office." Sometimes they find it necessary to "go to the top"—to place the problem before the general manager or the owner.

In a large rug factory daily visitors' tours were routed through the work area of a devout Christian girl. Since her department was, in a sense, on display, all the girls were expected to dress neatly and becomingly. To her immediate supervisor, the young believer dressed too modestly. If she did not "get with it," she would be replaced.

During the Wednesday evening prayer meeting the girl's pastor noticed that she was downcast—which was very unusual. When he asked why, she recounted her problem at work. The following day the pastor went "to the top." He made an appointment with the owner of the factory whom he knew quite well. He explained the situation. The owner thanked him and assured him he would "take care of it."

That afternoon the Christian girl was called to the front office. She went in fear and trembling. The owner greeted her kindly. "You look very neat and presentable," he commented.

"Well, thank you," the girl said.

The big man smiled. "Personally, I like your

appearance. I understand you have been ordered to follow the modern trend. Forget it. I appreciate Christian convictions. You have a job here as long as you want it."

Company policy was clarified because a godly girl lived her convictions; because her convictions and her problem were brought to top management.

To really learn what soul winning is all about, we must go to the Master, to Him "who is above all, and through all, and in you all" (Ephesians 4:6). Jesus said: "For the Son of man is come to seek and to save that which was lost. . . . Joy shall be in heaven over one sinner that repenteth, more than over ninety and nine just persons, which need no repentance" (Luke 19:10; 15:7). "As my Father hath sent me, even so send I you" (John 20:21). This is divine policy.

But the Lord goes further. He actually shows us how to win a soul.

The Master's Love

The first requisite is love. Jesus said, "For God so loved the *world*. . . ." That included Jews, Gentiles, and Samaritans.

After Israel was carried into captivity, the Assyrian king brought idolaters from Babylon and elsewhere, "and placed them in the cities of Samaria instead of the children of Israel" (2 Kings 17:24). These strangers intermarried with the Jews who remained in the land. Ancient writers referred to their offspring variously as "half-Jews" or "half-breed Israelites." They troubled the Hebrew remnant who later returned from Babylonian captivity. Strong animosity still existed between Jews and Samaritans during the time of Christ.

Although the most direct route from Judea to Galilee lay through Samaria, devout Jews would not take this way, feeling they would be defiled. They crossed the Jordan River, traveled north through Perea, and recrossed Jordan when they were beyond the borders of Samaria. But Jesus "must needs go through Samaria." He would have no part or lot in their feud.

In our day, many young people have become hippies— separated from the mainstream of society by unconventional habits, dress, and addiction to drugs. But thousands have found Jesus Christ and have come to be known as "Jesus People" or "Jesus Freaks." Changed by the power of God but turned off by religious form and the church, they worship in homes, empty storerooms—wherever they can. This segment of the younger generation and many of the older generation are at odds.

This ought not to be. The older generation needs some of the enthusiasm and zeal of the Jesus People. The young folks need the teaching the church can provide. Billy Graham said: "The big need for evangelicalism now is people who can ground the thousands of young converts in the knowledge of the Bible."

Soul winners today "must needs go through Samaria." They must entertain no prejudices. They must take the news to whosoever that God loves them, and then help the converts grow in grace.

How different are human souls? Are they not equally precious in the sight of God who is no respecter of persons?

The Master's Focus

Christ and His disciples entered Samaria and came to Jacob's Well at Sychar. While the Lord came to save a lost world, lost Jews, and lost Samaritans, His love focused on one needy woman. Just as He saw

Nathanael under the fig tree (John 1:48), He knew His path and the path of one sinful woman would cross.

Jesus sent His disciples to the city to buy food. He knew the condition of the woman coming to the well, and He wanted to minister to her without distraction or interruption. Christ had come to seek and save her.

If the disciples had remained at the well, surely some comment would have been made that would have put the Samaritan woman on the defensive. On a previous occasion they did not want Jesus to be bothered by parents bringing little children to Him. They even wanted to call down fire from heaven upon others.

Soul winning is an intensely personal meeting of saint and sinner; a meeting blessed by the brooding presence and guidance of the Holy Spirit. On the job, if another sinner approaches and makes some wise remark, the soul winner's prospect may become ill-at-ease. The mood of the moment can be broken and the opportunity lost.

It was noon in Sychar, a most unusual time to come to the well for water. But here in the heat of the day, a woman approached the well and Jesus. The necessity of coming alone was a constant reminder to her that she was ostracized by society. She was not proud, self-righteous, or boastful. She was a needy sinner.

Why is it that sick, burdened, and troubled people are the most likely ones to be won for Christ? Is it because we single them out?

The individual with money and friends who has all his heart's desires does not recognize his need. He turns us off, and we turn to the one who realizes his need of something or Someone. That's why there has been a great revival among the so-called hippies. They felt at odds with society. Rebellion, drugs, and permissiveness all failed to satisfy. They saw no reason for being. They were without hope. In desperation they turned to Jesus, and He took them as they were. No wonder they are zealous. No wonder they love Him!

The Master's Request

Jesus asked the woman of Samaria for a drink of water, something she could easily do—if she would.

One of the surest ways to get a person's attention is to ask a favor of him. If the request is one he can comply with without too much effort, he is usually happy to do it. The request places the petitioner under obligation to the other and may well open the door to further conversation.

Now the woman at the well could have become insolent. She could have made a few snide remarks about a well-bred Jew lowering himself to speak to a Samaritan. But the inference is that she began to draw water for Jesus and out of curiosity asked why He would make a request of her.

By asking Jesus this question, the woman opened the door to further conversation and gave the Lord opportunity to turn it into spiritual channels. Now Jesus offered to reciprocate. He said if she would only ask, He could give her living water.

The Reverend Andrew Maracle, an Indian himself, said that an Indian chief once gave Will Rogers a beautiful buckskin jacket. The famous humorist immediately unbuckled his gun belt and gave it and his treasured pearl-handled revolvers to the chief. He understood that to refuse the Indian's gift would be equivalent to a slap in the face. But to reciprocate was to make a covenant of everlasting friendship.

The "friend that sticketh closer than a brother" was offering a miraculous supply. It never occurred to the woman to doubt His sincerity. The gift of living water far surpassed the cup of water she had given. A short time before she had been anxious to get back to the privacy of her home. But now she was captivated by the words of the Master Soul Winner. Her distrust of people had been forgotten for the moment. She wanted to learn more about this living water.

After proving ourselves friendly, we must try to engage our prospect in conversation, a two-way exchange. We must endeavor to direct the conversation into spiritual channels. We must point out that Christ has a miraculous supply for the needs and longings of the human heart.

The Master's Knowledge

Now the divine supply of living water is available to whosoever will—with a qualification. He only can drink the cup of salvation who repents of his sin. So it was necessary for the woman's conscience to be awakened, for her to sense her guilt.

Jesus told His prospect to call her husband. When she said she had no husband, the Lord revealed His knowledge of her past and her present sinful condition. Embarrassed, she could have become angry. She didn't. On the other hand, Jesus could have said she was a hell-bound sinner. He didn't.

If it is at all possible, the soul winner must never antagonize a sinner. Solomon wrote: "A brother offended is harder to be won than a strong city" (Proverbs 18:19). And Gipsy Smith said, "It is easier to capture a city than to convert a soul." But even when a witness carefully plans his encounters with sinners, offense may be taken.

A Christian had witnessed to a fellow employee quite frequently. While he was eating lunch at his desk one day, the sinner approached and said, "So, you think just because I chew tobacco, cuss a little, and have a beer now and then that I'm going to hell. Well let me tell you—I'll have lots of company!"

The believer was so surprised words failed him. They had had no occasion to talk together that morning. He followed his sinner friend back through the shop. When he overtook the seemingly offended man, he said, "Davey, I didn't say that. Those things just go with a life apart from Christ. Rejection of Christ is the thing that sends men to hell."

The sinner smiled. "I know, buddy. I know. I was just checking." So they maintained their friendship and continued to talk about the love of God for erring men. And finally, Davey was converted. He was converted because the soul winner refused to be diverted from the main issue—what will you do with Jesus?

The Samaritan woman tried to engage Jesus in a controversy over the proper place to worship—Mount Gerizim or Jerusalem. The Lord pointed out that attitude rather than place was the vital consideration. Only those who worship God in Spirit and in truth worship Him acceptably.

The Master's Revelation

The conversation at Jacob's Well was leisurely. The woman did not try to break it off. Christ, with so many demands on His time, did not try to high-pressure her into an admission of guilt or a decision to ask how she could be forgiven. This gave her time to think. Probably she was pleased that a Jew of obviously good breeding chose to talk to her at length.

No doubt Jesus was unlike any other Jew she had met or heard about. There was something different about Him. What could His motive be? He was offering water—a well of water within, springing up into everlasting life. Yes, He was surely a prophet. But then she began to recall the prophecies.

"The woman saith unto him, I know that Messiah cometh, which is called Christ: when he is come, he will tell us all things. Jesus saith unto her, I that speak unto thee am he'' (John 4:25, 26).

A devout Christian took a course in soul winning. He remarked: "I did not have to read far into the book to realize it sounded like huckstering Jesus Christ from the produce wagon. We are not to sell our Jesus; we are to invite people to meet Him personally."

Jesus is coming soon. No one knows what a day may bring forth. We have no promise of a tomorrow. Sometimes we get greatly concerned. We wish our sinful friend would delay no longer. But it is *his* decision. He knows it, and he does not appreciate being pressured into it. Of his own free will he must accept or reject the Lord Jesus. So we must take time to talk, to listen, and to be friendly.

The more we talk and the oftener we consider together the call of Christ, the more the sinner will remember our testimony and our devotion to Christ. It will gradually permeate his thoughts that it must pay to serve Jesus. But in his mind the pleasures of sin may still outweigh the benefits of following the Lord.

If we keep steady, if we keep showing our concern for his soul, the sinner will finally realize that eternal life is more to be desired than the pleasures of sin for a season. The invitation of the eternal Son of God can no longer be denied.

How long will this take? One conversation? many conversations? a day? a year? ten years? as long as it takes the sinner to make a decision. Regardless of the time involved, we must not give up.

The Master Convinces

As Jesus finished saying He was the Messiah, His disciples returned. Surprised that He was talking with a Samaritan woman, they made no comments. Had Jesus been successful? Had He convinced the woman of her need? "By their fruits ye shall know them" (Matthew 7:20).

John 4:28 begins, "The woman then left . . .," so it is possible there was an interval of conversation between Jesus and the woman that is not recorded. However, it seems that Zaccheus was converted as he climbed down the tree. For when his feet hit the ground, he received Jesus joyfully and announced his plans to make restitution and to help the poor (Luke 19:1-10). The palsied man made no audible, recorded confession. But Jesus knew his thoughts and said: "Son, be of good cheer; thy sins be forgiven thee" (Matthew 9:2).

Knowing she was in the presence of the Messiah, the Samaritan woman probably repented and was converted before she left the well. Overjoyed, excited, and possessed with something more important than secular things, she left her waterpot and hurried into the city. She invited people to come and see One to whom her life was an open book—could He not be the Christ?

One evening a young woman (alone with her thoughts) began to recall the past, the years of Sunday school attendance and the more recent years of separation from any contact with spiritual things. The following day she met a Christian woman who bore testimony to her faith in Christ. Again the past unrolled before the mind's eye of the sinner. She tried to turn it off but could not. Realizing that a Third Party was present, she yielded to the soul winner's invitation and gave her heart to Christ.

When we "sent" ones by faith bring a soul into the presence of Jesus Christ and the sinner realizes that he is dealing with God, not man, he yields to the Saviour.

12
No Better Way

If the resurrection of Jesus Christ was a myth, then Saul of Tarsus was destined to go down in history with Moses and the prophets as a defender and preserver of the oracles of God. Devout and sincere, he was determined to thwart efforts of Christians to (as he supposed) turn people from Jehovah to Jesus of Nazareth, from the living oracles to the sayings of a dead man.

Having been instrumental in scattering the Christians from Jerusalem, he was not content. He witnessed against some who were put to death. And with authority from the chief priests he "persecuted them even unto strange cities" (Acts 26:11). He did it all because he loved God and His Word.

But Saul of Tarsus was destined to learn he was sincerely wrong. At midday as he neared Damascus with authority to imprison Christians, "a light from heaven, above the brightness of the sun" shone upon him and his companions. They fell to the ground, and Saul "heard a voice . . . saying in the Hebrew tongue, Saul, Saul, why persecutest thou me?" (vv. 12-14).

Saul knew this was not fantasy—God was speaking to him. He asked, "Who art thou, Lord?" And the answer came, "I am Jesus whom thou persecutest" (v. 15). Jesus of Nazareth was alive! He was God eternal!

"And he trembling and astonished said, Lord, what

wilt thou have me to do?'' (9:6). So saying, Saul yielded his soul, his life, his all to Jesus Christ. And it pleased Him who is above all "to reveal his Son in me [Saul], that I might preach him among the heathen" (Galatians 1:15, 16). There on the Damascus road Saul was changed from a vicious destroyer of Christianity to its most vigorous defender.

Billy Sunday was a Christian athlete—a daring, dashing player on the famous Chicago baseball team. When he felt the urge to serve God full time, he forsook worldly fame and threw all his zeal into Christian service. He became a great evangelist and won multiplied thousands to Christ.

Human zeal makes its mark in time. That zeal dedicated to Christ will be recorded in the annals of eternity.

There Are No Strangers

Saul was proud of his Hebrew heritage and background. He said: "I am . . . a Jew, born in Tarsus, a city in Cilicia, yet brought up in this city [Jerusalem] at the feet of Gamaliel, and taught according to the perfect manner of the law of the fathers, and was zealous toward God. . . . After the most straitest sect of our religion I lived a Pharisee . . ., believing all things which are written in the law and the prophets . . .; touching the righteousness which is in the law, blameless" (Acts 22:3; 26:5; 24:14; Philippians 3:6). He was the type that bypassed Samaria.

But after meeting Jesus, Paul said: "What things were gain to me, those I counted loss for Christ" (Philippians 3:7). He accepted Christ's call to "bear my name before the Gentiles, and kings, and the children of Israel" (Acts 9:15). No longer could he entertain respect of persons. Like his Master he could not take sides in any feud. He was "made all things to all men, that [he] might by all means save some" (1 Corinthians 9:22).

A church desired to support another missionary on the field. During a week of conferences they listened to the recommended candidate. The young woman was an excellent nurse, but she had no platform gifts. She did not sing or play a musical instrument. She was not a gifted speaker. How could she impress the people of the church?

Toward the end of the week the pastor visited among his congregation. In home after home even the children were enthused with their new missionary. "She is so Christlike. She just makes herself one of us," they said.

In her home church the prospective missionary was "all things to all men." She was a soul winner. So God promoted her to witness in a strange land.

The love of Christ constrained Paul to minister to Gentiles whom he had considered "aliens from the commonwealth of Israel, and strangers from the covenants of promise, having no hope, and without God in the world." And he could then say: "But now, in Christ Jesus, ye who sometime were far off are made nigh by the blood of Christ" (Ephesians 2:12, 13).

Focus on One

The Lord had told Ananias that "he [Paul] is a chosen vessel unto me . . . I will show him how great things he must suffer for my name's sake" (Acts 9:15, 16). Resisted by Elymas the sorcerer in Paphos. Expelled from Antioch in Pisidia. Stoned and left for dead in Lystra. Paul did not give up. He was a determined and dedicated man.

When Paul ministered in Philippi, he was beaten with many stripes and secured in stocks in the inner prison. "At midnight Paul and Silas prayed, and sang praises unto God: and the prisoners heard them" (Acts

109

16:25). What a testimony! They believed Jesus who had said: "Blessed are ye, when men shall . . . persecute you . . . for my sake. Rejoice, and be exceeding glad" (Matthew 5:11, 12).

Then an earthquake rocked the prison. All the doors opened; and everyone's shackles dropped off. Awaking and supposing the prisoners had escaped, the jailor was about to commit suicide. Paul shouted, "Do thyself no harm."

Then to the jailor's question ("What must I do to be saved?"), Paul replied: "Believe on the Lord Jesus Christ, and thou shalt be saved, and thy house" (Acts 16:30, 31). Jesus was concerned about individuals, their homes, and their cities. Here, Paul led the jailor and his family to Christ.

A husband and wife reached the parting of the ways. She kept the four children, and he began to travel as a salesman. In a motel one day he picked up a Bible and began to read. Conviction came upon him, and he yielded to Christ. Immediately he began to pray for his family.

That same day his children attended a Bible-story hour and were converted. Enthusiastically, they told their mother that Jesus was living in their hearts. She too accepted Him. And the family was reunited.

When the love of God becomes real to the heart of a person, he begins to think of those he loves—the ones who are unsaved. And he desires that they come to know his Saviour too.

Friendly Approach

At Salamis, Antioch in Pisidia, and Iconium, Paul went into the synagogues and preached. He went "to the Jew first." Then in a vision he saw a man of Macedonia appealing, "Come over into Macedonia, and help us" (Acts 16:9). Gathering that God was calling him, Paul and his companions finally arrived in Philippi.

There was no synagogue in the city. They received no welcome, no further guidance from the Spirit. They "were in that city abiding certain days"—*marking time.* Inquiries brought out the fact that a prayer service was held by a river on the Sabbath. It turned out to be a small gathering of women. If Paul was disappointed, there is no indication of it in the Scriptures.

Jesus "must needs go" through Samaria to seek and to save a needy woman. Paul was called to Philippi to minister to a Gentile woman (Lydia) who knew there was a true and living God. She prayed to Him but did not know about His forgiveness of sins.

Like the woman of Samaria, Lydia recognized her spiritual need and the divine invitation. She accepted Christ and was baptized. Now she considered it a small thing to favor God's messengers and to lodge them in her home. Her home became a meeting place, and in this friendly atmosphere souls were born into the Kingdom. Later Paul "went out of the prison, and entered into the house of Lydia: and when they had seen the brethren, they comforted them, and departed" (v. 40).

One summer a student minister canvassed the area in a rural home-mission field. Late in the day he came to a farm and received a gracious invitation to have supper in the home. At the table father, mother, and three children joined voices singing:

"For health and strength and daily food,

We give thee thanks, O Lord."

So he was in a Christian home.

During pleasant conversation after the meal, the young soul winner learned they belonged to different denominations. However, his host's church was served by a minister only once a month. The entire family was pleased to learn their visitor planned to conduct a Vacation Bible School. They assured him of their cooperation and paved the way for his acceptance and ministry in that part of the vineyard. Christian friendship aided in the effort to win souls.

Conviction a Necessity

On the Island of Cyprus, Paul and his co-workers came to Paphos. Sergius Paulus, governor of the island, asked Paul to preach the gospel before him. He was a prudent, intelligent man who believed there was more to life than pleasure, honor, and success. Having found no satisfaction in religion, he had turned to one who claimed magical powers, Elymas the sorcerer.

In ancient times it was not unusual for influential political figures to retain wise men and magicians in their households or courts. Pharaoh had magicians. Nebuchadnezzar depended on astrologers and wise men.

Elymas realized that if Sergius Paulus accepted Christ, his position and hope of personal gain were gone. So he probably tried to discredit the missionaries by mocking and criticizing them. This ungodly Jew was keeping an inquiring soul from learning that sin separates man from a loving God. He was fighting against God. Under the inspiration of the Holy Spirit, Paul pronounced judgment (blindness) upon him for a season (Acts 13:4-12).

A college professor delighted in undercutting the belief of his students in the existence of God. Finally a student raised his hand and said, "Sir, we admire your intelligence and insight. How much of all the knowledge in the world do you think you possess?"

After moments of thought, the professor replied to this loaded question: "Oh, about three percent."

Then came the clincher from the student. "If that is

so, don't you think possibly God may exist somewhere in the ninety-seven percent you don't know?"

However, the mocker can also be squelched by a meek and quiet spirit. A godly nurse secured employment in a large city hospital where she faithfully witnessed to her fellow employees. Although some seed fell in good ground, she soon became aware of resentment on the part of a middle-aged nurse who had been at the hospital for many years. Finally, this woman ridiculed her publicly in the lunchroom. She concluded, "I can't get you fired, and I can't get you mad enough to quit. What's the matter with you?"

The soul winner quietly replied, "Christ takes the sting out of the things you say because He loves me. I have been praying daily for you because I know He loves you too."

The elderly nurse departed in haste, but later that day she apologized. And in the supply room the soul winner led her to Christ.

Sinners Need an Introduction

Paul said, "We preach Christ crucified" (1 Corinthians 1:23). He introduced men to Jesus Christ, their Saviour and Lord.

In Antioch he preached that "God, according to his promise, raised unto Israel a Saviour, Jesus." But dwellers in Jerusalem and their rulers did not recognize Him of whom their prophets wrote. And they fulfilled the prophecies by condemning Jesus to death on the cross. "But God raised him from the dead. . . . Be it known unto you therefore, men and brethren, that through this man is preached unto you the forgiveness of sins" (Acts 13:23-28). Many forsook their sins and believed in a living, powerful Saviour.

Fourteen years after leaving his home a man was genuinely converted. God gave him a real love for his family so he went back for a visit. His mother did not know him; he had to introduce himself to her. But above all, he wanted to introduce her to Jesus Christ. How well he remembered—none of them had ever attended Sunday school or church. Mother had no knowledge of God and no desire for spiritual realities.

Then his mother became seriously ill. As she lay in the hospital near death, he talked to her about One who could meet the need of her soul and forgive her. He gave his personal testimony—what Christ had done for him. But she did not know how to pray. "Jesus is here," the young Christian said. "Just talk to Him as you do to me."

Haltingly, she began to talk to the Lord and then stopped. "Son, I'm sorry I haven't been the kind of mother I should have," she said.

The godly son soothed her and encouraged her to pray. She did. She came to know Jesus who died to deliver her from all sin. "I feel His presence," she said. "I'm ready to go now. I'm not afraid."

Jesus introduced himself to the woman of Samaria. This was the chief business of Paul and every soul winner since—to introduce unsaved people to Jesus Christ who alone can save them and give them peace here and hereafter.

Effort to Convince

Jesus convinced the Samaritan woman of her need of His grace and forgiveness. Paul convinced Sergius Paulus, Lydia, the Philippian jailor, and many others of their need of the Saviour. He taught. He reasoned. Many times he recounted his personal experience in Jesus Christ.

On two particular occasions Paul knew he was going to have one opportunity—and only one—to witness and to convince souls for whom Christ died: before the mob that tried to kill him in Jerusalem (Acts 21:27 through 22:23) and before King Agrippa (26:1-29).

It was more than preaching, more than logic. It was the heartfelt account of his personal encounter with Jesus Christ. It was a narrative that would stay with them and prick their hearts upon every remembrance of Paul.

Men who raised their voices to cry for the crucifixion of Christ, still yielded to the voice of the Holy Spirit on the Day of Pentecost and were saved. And only God knows how many of those who raised their voices against Paul, who listened to his defense, finally believed in Jesus Christ.

Well-educated, grounded in the Scriptures, enlightened by an abundance of divine revelations—yet Paul consistently used his personal testimony effectively.

How very fortunate is the soul winner who is converted in his youth. He can minister to the youth of this troubled era. Jesus Christ remains unchanged. Desire and repentance opened the door then, and they still do. The grace of God has been sufficient throughout the years, and it still is.

Jesus did not convince everyone to whom He spoke. Paul did his best, under God, but he was rejected sometimes. Jesus and Paul sowed Spirit-inspired words in the hearts of hearers that could later produce a harvest. So can we.

13
Your World

Where You Are

God so loved the world that He gave His Son. One day Jesus wept over Jerusalem saying: "How often would I have gathered thy children together, even as a hen gathereth her chickens under her wings, and ye would not!" (Matthew 23:37). Christ yearned for all men everywhere to come unto Him and be saved. He said: "The field is the world. . . . Lift up your eyes, and look on the fields; for they are white already to harvest" (Matthew 13:38; John 4:35).

However, the Lord's earthly ministry and travels covered but a minute portion of the earth. The revelation of the love, compassion, and power of God; the death and resurrection of Christ; the coming of the Holy Spirit on the Day of Pentecost—this had all become a reality to a relatively small number of people at the ascension of Christ. Physically, the Lord could not and did not minister to the entire whitened harvest field.

The apostle Paul traveled much more extensively, but he did not preach to the world. Although the field is the world, it begins in the home and extends to the neighborhood, to school, to work, and to the town, before it extends to the far corners of the earth.

Sow the seed where you are. Jesus did. Paul did. Everyone should "abide in the same calling wherein he was called" (1 Corinthians 7:20), faithfully witnessing to those he contacts. He should go to other fields of labor only as the Holy Spirit moves him. (See Acts 13:2.)

Charles Trumbull, mighty soul winner of a past generation, said: "The world is never going to be brought to Christ wholesale, but one by one. Men are not born collectively; they do not die collectively; they do not accept Christ collectively. The harvest must be hand-picked."*

And Christ said: "Pray ye therefore the Lord of the harvest, that he will send forth laborers into his harvest" (Matthew 9:38). You in your small corner and I in mine, that the field may be reaped.

So Ready

Some pray for those who have not heard the story of Jesus and His love. Many give that the gospel may be preached in all the world for a witness. Few reach the regions beyond with the gospel. But this worldwide vision of multitudes to be reaped should spur us to action.

A Midwestern banker once managed many farms. During the spring and fall, he hired crews to plant and to reap. Driving through the region one spring day, he came upon a whole field of unreaped grain. It had been planted the previous year and the grain had matured well by harvesttime, but somehow he had overlooked that field. Now it was too late.

Likewise, the soul winner cannot reap the field he does not see. One may be aware of the far-flung fields and yet overlook the field at hand.

A teacher of junior boys for many years requested a transfer to the adult women's Bible class. For several weeks different Christians substituted in the boys'

Pentecostal Evangel, May 5, 1966.

class. Then a capable young man assumed the regular teaching assignment. Six months later he resigned in despair.

Among those who again substituted in the boys' class was a rather quiet young Christian. He knew only too well that he was not as gifted as the former teachers. But his heart went out to the active, mischievous youngsters. He wondered what they thought as they listened to adult Christians testify of their devotion to the Lord Jesus. Perhaps the boys wondered how these adults could love Christ whom they had not seen and fail to be concerned about those they saw almost every week.

The diffident one volunteered to teach the boys. Oh, he learned how mischievous they could be. He prayed. He prepared. Sometimes on Sunday afternoons he wept as he reviewed the lesson and prepared for the next one. But he never thought of giving up. He loved those boys, and they began to realize it.

It took time. Months passed before one of his pupils accepted Jesus as his Saviour. But within a year they were all in the fold. Christ said: "Suffer the little children to come unto me." No field is so ready for the harvest as the hearts of children.

Keep Your Vineyard

Early Christians faithfully ministered in their homes and from house to house. They "filled Jerusalem with [their] doctrine" (Acts 5:28). Then great persecution scattered them abroad, and they "went every where preaching the word" (8:1-4). They began in Jerusalem and then went "unto the uttermost part of the earth" (1:8).

The prophet Samuel had an extensive ministry. Dedicated to God before he was born, he eventually brought victory to his defeated people. He judged Israel the remainder of his life, riding circuit throughout the land.

But somehow Samuel failed in the ministry closest to him—in the home. "His sons walked not in his ways, but turned aside after lucre, and took bribes, and perverted judgment" (1 Samuel 8:3). Perhaps the old prophet cried, "Mine own vineyard have I not kept" (The Song of Solomon 1:6).

Saved at an early age, a man married and reared a son. That boy was brought up in church. He saw and experienced the faithfulness of his parents in church and in support of the church's outreach. Converted in his teens, when he became a man he decided to travel the way of his own choosing.

Many times the parents wept and talked and wondered where and how they had failed. The mother suggested that they had been too strict. The father always replied, "Now, honey, if we had it to do all over again, you know we would live as we have." They had won souls to Christ, but their own son was not in the fold.

Eventually, the day came when the son (now a father himself) visited his parents. "Dad, if you can't help me, I don't know what I'm going to do," he said. The elderly parents listened to a heart-wrenching story of the problems and fears of their boy. Then the old gentleman said quietly, "Son, I can't help you, but Jesus can. Let's pray together."

There was a harvest that day in the home. Early the following morning the phone rang. It was their son. "Dad," he cried, "Jesus is real. He even took the fear of death away."

The Harvest Is Great

Jesus "ordained twelve, that they should be with him, and that he might send them forth to preach"

119

(Mark 3:14). He sent the Twelve and then the Seventy saying: "The harvest truly is great, but the laborers are few: pray ye therefore the Lord of the harvest, that he would send forth laborers into his harvest" (Luke 10:1, 2).

Jesus was concerned about the great harvest field; concerned about the paucity of laborers to reap the harvest. He sent forth whom He could and those who would. The number of reapers multiplied in the Early Church, and multitudes were gathered from the whitened harvest field.

By A.D. 100, Christianity had been proclaimed in most large cities of the Mediterranean world. In the Apostolic Era as many as ½ million converts were won to Christ. During the next 200 years intense persecution only served to increase the Church in numbers.

Then Emperor Constantine accepted Christianity, and it became Rome's official religion. The historian Gibbon says Christians numbered not more than 5 percent of the subjects of the Roman Empire. Others have given estimates of up to 50 percent. Nevertheless, never in history has a religious faith peacefully achieved such enormous growth in such a short time.

Multiplied thousands are being won to Christ in our day. But the harvest is still great, and the laborers are few. The world is by no means Christian, and it becomes less Christian day by day. World population increases while the proportionate number of Christians decreases.

In 1950, Christians were about 33 percent of the world population. Ten years later they had dropped to 31 percent. If this rate of decline continues, by A.D. 2000, Christians will be about 20 percent. Christ and the apostles recognized the enormity of the field and task. So do we, and by the grace of God we are determined that the gates of hell shall not prevail against the Church.

While statistics and population figures are important, they are also cold and impersonal. It takes something more to kindle desire to win the lost. The realization of the condition of the field, the condition of lost souls, inspires soul-winning activity.

Jesus said the lost are as sheep without a shepherd (Matthew 9:36). He was moved with compassion. He sought them. He gave himself unstintingly to bring them into the fold.

Driving along a country road, a Christian saw what appeared to be the flailing of an animal's feet far out in the field. Curious, he went to the scene and found a sheep on its back in a small hollow or depression. Desperately, it was trying to right itself. It needed assistance. If the Christian or someone else had not rolled the little animal off its back, it could well have died. And if someone does not come to the aid of lost souls, they will die without Christ.

It was happening in church—in a college-age Sunday school class. Unquestionably, the dedicated teacher had made every pupil feel that he or she was important and loved. But the time came when signs of restlessness and disinterest began to crop up.

One Sunday the teacher began by saying how sorry he was and what an apology he owed them. Surprised, the class gave him rapt attention. With tears coursing down his cheeks, the teacher told them how he loved them. Saddened to see interest waning and attendance decreasing, he had prayed all week. Although his heart ached for their souls, somehow he must have failed them.

Those young people knew that godly man well. They

121

knew how difficult it was for him to bare the agony of his soul. The Holy Spirit began to convict them of their indifference, lukewarmness, and sin. One by one they slipped to their knees. The resulting revival spread through the entire church. Straying and lost sheep entered the fold because one man came to the rescue in prayer and tears and testimony; because one man evidenced love and compassion such as only Christ can inspire.

Only in Christ

Multitudes are without Christ. Though a man have culture, education, position, wealth, and have not Christ, he has nothing. "If any man be in Christ, he is a new creature" and heir to eternal promises (2 Corinthians 5:17). Only in Christ is a man secure.

A Christian's employer decided to send him away for 10 weeks of schooling. Although the prospective student did not like the idea, he knew he could drive the 160 miles to school every Monday morning and return Friday evening. By taking his quarterly along he could study and keep teaching his Sunday school class. Still there was a "why?" deep in his soul.

The following day he received a phone call. A young man from another company was slated to take the same course for 5 weeks. He suggested that they travel together and share expenses. It was agreed, and midway on their first trip conversation ceased. The Christian's young companion attended church, but he was not interested in talking "religion." However, conversation resumed 50 miles or so later, and by the time they arrived they were friends.

The men secured a room in the home of a widow who catered to students. Since they were going to sleep in the same room, attend the same school, and perhaps eat in the same restaurants, the Christian decided to "cool it" religiously. If 5 weeks of living the Christian life before his unconverted friend did not bring him to Christ, then no amount of "preaching" could do it.

Seldom does a Christian have such an opportunity. The believer bowed his head over his food in the restaurants, read his Bible and studied his Sunday school lessons, and prayed in his friend's presence. On the 2nd day the sinner was asking what the Christian believed—and why. He soon knew that church attendance does not necessarily make one a Christian. And during the 2nd week he received Christ as his Saviour. What a blessed time of fellowship they had for the remaining weeks of school!

Hopeless Without Christ

Self-righteous people trust in their good deeds and in the fact that they are "not as other men are, extortioners, unjust, adulterers . . ." (Luke 18:11). Others just brush the thought of eternity from their mind hoping it will all "turn out right in the end." But all have sinned. And the wages of sin is death. Apart from Christ, all men are lost; all sinners are without hope.

A young man in the hospital had but a short time to live. Several years before one kidney had been removed, and the other had now failed. Ministers and Christian friends had tried to help him, but to all he said, "I promised to serve God several times in my life, but I always reneged on my promise. I'm lost. I'm lost."

Finally, a friend came in with a godly layman. Noting the Bible in the visitor's hand, the dying youth cried, "Don't try to preach to me. I failed God. I'm eternally lost." And he told the story of his broken vows to God.

Quietly the newcomer said, "I know how you feel. I understand."

Almost fiercely the desperate sinner turned on him: "How can you? No one understands."

Then the visitor explained how it felt to be in the army, in combat. To put your life in jeopardy moment by moment, day after day. To see one after another of your buddies die. And to feel it is only a question of time until the bullet marked with your name reaches its mark.

Then to come home. To have employment in the old job deferred month after month. To have too much time to think. To become depressed. To feel no one cared—not even the Lord. In this condition years passed before he realized anew that God is love, and that He casts no one out who comes to Him in prayer. The Christian concluded, "In desperation I prayed and kept on praying. Christ received me. He delivered me from doubt, depression, and fear. He forgave me."

The dying youth said, "You really do understand!" Hope arose in his heart. What Christ had done for his visitor, He could do for him. The lost sheep came into the fold.

If someone does not come to the rescue of a lost soul, he will die without Christ.

Wrapping It Up

You are unique, different. No one has experienced identical trials and problems. In your own individual way you have learned from defeat and have risen to conquer. By faith you have obtained divine guidance and help. "He [God] helps us in all our troubles, so that we are able to help those who have all kinds of troubles, using the same help that we ourselves have received from God" (2 Corinthians 1:4, TEV). You have something special to offer sin-burdened people.

No one has the same circle of acquaintances you have. You wield an influence for good over some people

124

that absolutely no one else does. God can use you to accomplish what would be impossible for others. This is not because you are an outstanding personality, but rather because God turns the wheels of circumstance. He helps you minister to the right person at the right time.

Nevertheless, the unbeliever must be willing. No sinner can be saved unless he cooperates with the soul winner and with the Lord.

Above all, in every encounter between witness and sinner, the Holy Spirit must guide one and convict the other. He brings it all together and draws the lost one into the fold.

It takes three to win a soul to Christ: a soul winner, a willing sinner, and the Holy Spirit.

To be one with God and be inspired by the Holy Spirit to win the lost—this is the most satisfying and rewarding labor a Christian can know.